NEW WAYS IN SEX EDUCATION

Books by Dorothy W. Baruch

A GUIDE FOR PARENTS

AND TEACHERS

new
ways
in sex
education

DOROTHY WALTER BARUCH, Ph.D.

Sketches by LOIS FISHER

Technical drawings by
ROBERT DEMAREST

McGraw-Hill Book Company, Inc.

NEW YORK   TORONTO   LONDON

NEW WAYS IN SEX EDUCATION

First Edition

To Hy
who knows so surely that
feelings come first

Acknowledgments

I am grateful—
To Louise Zabriskie for permission to translate into drawings some of the photographs on birth from her book *Mother and Baby Care* (Lippincott, 1953), which I have used successfully many times with children . . .

To *National Parent-Teacher* for permission to quote in Chapter 13 from an article in its February, 1957, issue called "Becoming Sensitive to Children's Fears," and to the group of truly sensitive teachers who wrote it out of experiences in their classrooms—Jewel Goldberg, Dolores Heideman, Darwin North, Doris Patterson, Ferne Smidderks, and Ann Younger . . .

And once more to the group of teachers above, and also to Kenneth McLean, Joan Schoolmaster, and Amy Mathews, for the various descriptions of work they carried on with artistry and insight . . .

To Martin Grotjahn, who gave generously of time and mind in the middle of his busy and productive life . . .

To Eileen Reynolds, whose cheerfulness, patience, and perseverence in typing this manuscript were matched by her swiftness and consummate skill . . .

To Alathena Kasten and Esther Bogart for helping out at the end with cooperative spirits and willing hands . . .

To Annie Bell Jackson, who saved me many moments for writing by her thoughtful attention . . .

To the colleagues and parents who waded through the material in its various stages of disorder and who gave me their honest criticisms which, I hope, helped the final writing come closer to meeting parents' and teachers' needs . . .

And most of all—to the parents and children who contributed their experiences, feelings, and thoughts. . . .

Contents

3 | SEX EDUCATION THAT GROWS WITH YOUR CHILD

How to Get the Most out of This Book
(Important Note: PLEASE DON'T SKIP!)

In today's sex education there is still much that only yesterday we feared to face and talk about.

An honest book on sex education today is, therefore, bound to contain some complex and—yes—disturbing or shocking aspects.

But parents and teachers (and others interested in the sex education of children and young people today) are tired of having certain parts of the problem marked "taboo" and left out.

And so, because I have faith in today's parents and teachers, and because I have seen, in working with them over many years, that they have intelligence and courage and the capacity to take things straightforwardly—I have included such matters in this book.

I think and hope that I have put these in a way that makes sense. It has not been easy. I believe, however, that as it stands the ideas lead logically one into the next, so that if you read the whole book without skipping parts of it, ideas that might otherwise remain puzzling, will come clear.

We are human.

Our children are human.

Human beings are born out of sexual union. They are heir to sexual expression and experiencing—able or not to reach the ultimate integration of sex with love.

The goal is not simple. In reaching it, a child goes through varying stages in his development. These stages, however, are not tightly bounded by age. One eleven-year-old may be very much an "adolescent," another very much a child. Actually no age or stage is separated from any other. Where one stops and the other begins cannot be marked out like a county line. One merges into the next. Each leads forward to all others; each goes back to one that existed before. There is the infant in every grown-up. There is the two-year-old and the three-

There is some of the child in every adult.

year-old and the thirteen- and eighteen-year-old in every adult.

It is this way: To do long division we must have gone through subtraction, multiplication, short division. . . . These are so automatically incorporated into the process that one does not often stop to think of them as parts. And yet, without them we are lost. We cannot do what is expected. We are stuck.

Some people do get stuck in infancy; some at the two- or four-year-old level. But most of us are what we are—a combination of all levels.

Life flows back and forth with fantasies and feelings and strivings from infancy or from when one was two or three or four or five. Even when one cannot remember these, they influence how one loves at twenty or forty or sixty. From each age and stage we put into our mental wallets a kind of essential coinage to use later. And when *later* arrives we go back to *earlier* to complete the wherewithal to gain and accomplish what it is we want now.

This may sound mysterious. It will, however, become more real to you as you move on. But for this to happen, it's important to take things in order.

So please, in reading this book—

Do not skip

You may want to. If, for instance, your child is an adolescent, you will naturally have the urge to turn at once to the part on adolescence. But don't. Instead, start at the beginning.

As you read about infants, think back on how it was with your child as an infant. In your mind's eye follow him through each stage of development, using what you read as a kind of guide to your thinking. This will help you see why your child is as he is now.

Review what you did earlier. Search out mistakes of the past, but not to mourn over them. Mistakes are human. Every parent makes them. However, *awareness of mistakes in the past often brings the opportunity to make up for them in the present.*

Look back on yourself too and on your own feelings.

No matter how old the children are in whom you are interested, follow this same plan.

This is not a book of recipes. Sex is too deeply a matter of individual feeling. In this book you will find many general suggestions. But in using any of them, *you will need to adapt it to your own individuality and taste.* You cannot take one ingredient and another and mix them together and come out with a dish that is universally digestible. You cannot measure out feelings according to any set of directions. Some of the ideas you will come upon will seem undigestible to you, perhaps even revolting. Others will be palatable. Some you will reject. Some you will use. But whatever you choose, use it in your own way, according to what seems good for *you.*

This is not a book of prescriptions, although you will find many principles to apply as you wish. This is rather a book of facts and of the experiences which parents and teachers and others who have worked closely with children have had. It is a book of children talking out of their wisdom, their wonderings, and their trembling and zealous wish to know more—in their hearts, not alone in their minds.

This is a book of *leads.* For you to mull over. For you to explore. For you to *test out.*

Some of these new ways in sex education you will find yourself already aware of. Others will contain more of discovery. You may begin to see, as parts of sex education, things you never before realized belonged! All told, it is hoped they will help you gain more sensitive understandings both about your children and yourself.

PART 1 | FROM PAST TO PRESENT: BASIC UNDERSTANDINGS

1 | Being Married Is Part of Sex Education

Loving and Being Together

Mary and Tom had just had a baby. Today Mary had come home from the hospital, a great deal thrilled, a little bit weepy.

"He's so tiny," she said to Tom. "How can a person like you or me grow from such a little thing?"

That night, as they lay in bed together, Tom thought of the hours at the hospital. He'd paced. Read, and not seen what he was reading. Started cup after cup of tasteless coffee. All through the hours, he'd kept thinking: Women don't die from having babies. Not any more.

He'd tried to hang onto that thought. And he'd breathed a sigh of relief every time the doctor had come out to tell him that Mary was doing beautifully. "She's as healthy as they make them. Not a thing to worry about!"

But no sooner would the doctor disappear than the worry would fill him once again. He'd known it was senseless. And yet there it was. And with it a curious thing had happened. He kept hearing an echo of his mother's voice saying what she'd said so often when he was a child: "When you were born . . . it almost killed me." And now the thought of any woman . . . of Mary's having a baby . . . still carried with it an unrealistic fear out of that past.

He thought of his mother and father. He had never seen on

his mother's face the wide-open smile of greeting that Mary gave him when he stepped through the door in the evening. His parents were even-tempered and kindly, but somehow aloof. He'd never even seen them kiss.

Why? he asked himself. After all, was it shameful to love? Why had it been so hard for him to be open in his feelings? Why did embarrassment always creep in?

Mary would say: "You never tell me you love me."

"I don't have to; I do."

"You don't show it enough."

"But," Tom would tease with the lightness he generally used to cover his embarrassment, "but, Mary dear, we're married, and married people can't make love all their lives!"

"Why can't they?"

"I," lamely, "I don't know."

When Mary had started to have the baby, the doctor had told Tom that during pregnancy and for a while after the birth of a child, a woman needed particularly large doses of affection. He knew this. But still he couldn't give it. Something inside him, stronger than knowledge, continued to influence what he did.

He could see it now. His difficulty in sharing feelings had come out of his past. For one thing, his mother and father had never shared theirs. Nor had either of them ever told him anything about sex. He'd resented that terribly. . . .

He'd have to do better for his son.

Close beside him Mary lay with eyes open. The fear she'd felt in the hospital still sent small chills through her. She told herself: Be sensible, Mary. It's all over.

In the delivery room the doctor had repeated, "Take it easy." He'd understood that it was natural to be afraid. All girls were, at least a little. But not that much. Almost panic. Not only during labor. Curiously, the worst panic had come later. The first time she'd gotten out of bed. As she stood up, she'd had the awful sensation: Everything was going to drop out! The doctor had reassured her she was all right. She knew she was. But still, nonsensically, she'd almost fainted from fear. . . .

As she thought of this now in bed beside Tom, a far more ancient thought intruded itself. Unaccountably she heard her mother saying to the little child Mary, "You'll hurt yourself." . . . For what reason had her mother kept repeating that? Oh yes, she remembered. It was because of the way she had insisted on climbing onto the top bar of the fence, straddling it to get those sensations she'd liked. . . .

Mary shut her eyes and her mind returned to her marriage and how she had taken so long to get over the unfounded fear that Tom would hurt her. . . . But why should these ridiculous old feelings keep cropping up now? And suddenly a tiny new spearhead of fear went through her: Would Tom hurt her when he wanted her again?

Once more her thoughts ran back to her childhood: After her father had gone, how she had wished for someone to fill his boots. She'd followed the big boy next door around like an adoring puppy until that day when her mother chanced upon her watching in thrilled fascination while the boy stood urinating in the alley behind their house. Mary had been excited, delighted, and entranced until her mother appeared.

Her mother had been furious at her. And inside herself, Mary had been furious in return. The same sort of fury that would sweep into her now at Tom over foolish little occurrences that didn't warrant so much fury. To this very day, however, she had never shown it. In spite of her wonderful doctor's saying, "It's not good, Mary, to hold your anger in so tightly!" she'd kept it back just as she had always done with her mother. But, even so, that awful sense of being "bad" had spread to so many things!

Of course her mother had had to let her know that you just couldn't do everything you wanted. But she hadn't needed to

5

make her feel like such a monster for having been interested. ... The teacher with whom Mary had taken a course for new mothers during her pregnancy had talked of how parents could handle this sort of episode quietly and definitely but without condemning a child for his natural interest in sex. And this thought had clicked.

On the other hand, Mary recalled, her mother had told her everything—everything she'd asked. But there had been so many things she hadn't asked. Silly things one imagined but never talked of, they'd seemed so senseless. ... And yet, last month the teacher had made the point: Sometimes it was the imaginary, senseless, and unspoken thoughts that kept you from being sensible far too long. ...

Her little baby with his life just starting! She and Tom together would do better for him.

In the dark she turned toward Tom and whispered with a half-giggle rising, "Isn't he the homeliest baby?"

"Why, you silly, wonderful idiot!" He wiped the tears from her cheeks. "He's beautiful, darling, like you—and like me, too!" And for once there was no embarrassment or levity in it, but rather the mingling of revelation and reverence rounding his voice.

He kissed her gently. "Last time I held you here in my arms, we didn't know whether we were having a boy or a girl."

"But we learned when it happened," with warm content.

Improving on What Happened to Us

Actually one rarely learns *all* about anything beforehand. Mary and Tom had learned about sex, not only by many things that had gone before but also by loving and being together. But the useless doubts, the foolish yet persistent and insistent intrusion of groundless fears, of hesitation, of anger too great for the occasion that sparked it—these had stood in the way of their reaching readily the deepest parts of what each wanted to learn. Old feelings from the past had made it hard to be easy together when it could have been simple and right. . . .

This is the aim of sex education: to find full-hearted and full-bodied satisfactions in mature and warm mutuality, securely entered into and happily complete.

**The END and AIM
of sex education
is developing one's FULLEST
CAPACITY for LOVE.**

From out of the past come feelings that help and feelings that hinder.

To help positive feelings grow high—
To help negative feelings stay low—
Both of these are important.

In the sex education of our children, we need to pay attention to both.

2 | The A B C's of Sex Education

Sex Education Is Far More than Sex Information

Over the years we have come to realize that the giving of sex information is not all there is to sex education. Sex education is a much broader, more complex, and many-sided thing. A mother's attitude toward herself when she menstruates, a father's toward his daughter's maturing, the shrugging off or the welcome with which one of them greets the other's kiss— all of these tell about sex. Through innuendoes, through looks of delight or astonishment, feigned innocence or aggravation, we tell a lot; not only through words.

If we say nothing at all to our children, they still acquire notions about sex. *Our very silence tells them something:* What is this hushed and secret thing? Is it strange? Unwanted? "Bad"?

Many EXPERIENCES
and NOT ALONE WHAT IS TOLD him
enter into a child's
sex education.

This is quite clear.

And so we will not want the information-giving part of sex education to take over so much of our attention that we lose sight of the whole. We will not want to leave the other parts of sex education so much to chance.

It is true that many of us have been doing many of the things that help children most. But we've been doing them unwittingly, without knowing that they were a part of the picture. We are much like the bright ten-year-old who, in a class discussion on how to make and keep friends, exclaimed, "Oh, I've done that before but by accident, not knowing what I was doing. And when you don't know what you're doing, you're apt either to overdo it or you don't do it as strong as you should. And then sometimes when you don't mean to, you slip up."

When we know more about what goes into sex education, we can be surer and stronger in what we do. We can avoid some of the slip-ups. We can reach more positive ends.

As an initial step, then, we will want to ask: Of what does sex education more broadly consist?

All-important Essentials

Let us look at the fundamentals—the *A B C*'s of sex education—those things by which a child comes to learn about sex. For convenience we can classify them under three headings: *Attachments. Body Sensitivities. Concepts.* These intertwine and overlap. Taken together they are all-important.

"A" IS FOR ATTACHMENTS   We hope we can help our children arrive at a place where each is able to form a vital, fully rounded, and significant attachment to a person of the opposite sex, gaining and giving many and varied satisfactions.

Sex is man and woman, and all each contains, brought to the other. But sex can also be man and woman, each struggling alone and apart to get from the other what each feels has been missed.

Sex can be the highest and the smoothest place of going, the utmost of being together, the least of loneliness any human being can find. But sex can also be agony and wanting. Hurting

9

and being hurt. And the endless waiting for what never is reached.

Sex can be warm and generous. But, in contrast, it can be a drab and ugly, stingy little offering, faintly stretched forth, weakly proffered, fearingly begrudged.

Sex can be of togetherness in love—or of hate that holds people attached.

But none of these feelings springs full-grown like Eve out of the rib of Adam. They start at the very beginning of life.

"Just think! His sex education's already begun."

Every child's sexual-emotional development most desirably moves along in an orderly sequence of attachments. In brief, he focuses first on mother. His attachment to her is the one most vital to him. Gradually he moves to a greater necessity for a meaningful attachment with father. And this is differently shaped according to whether the child is a boy or a girl. When brothers and sisters are present, his attachments to them have

10

bearing on his sex education. Still later, his attachment to adults outside the family and to his peers and his peer group increase in importance. And finally he focuses on one member of the opposite sex.

This does not mean, however, that his mother and father have become worthless to him. The fact is that his relationship with them carries over into the whole of his life and can contribute very positive values and strengths.

Anne writes to her sweetheart, "It was my father and my mother, I think, who showed me the way to the tenderness you love in me. There was something stalwart, you might say, in how they were with us and with each other. Not always easy, though. My mother would get spells of fussy excitement and my father was stormy at times. But there was an essential balance. I remember so many things: A day when I was small, soon after my baby brother was born. I felt blue and had crept into a corner, and my mother came and swept me up and rocked me and sang and spoke gently of my nose being out of joint. She played a little pantomime of putting it back on straight. But the moment had no mockery in it. It was wistfully serious. She knew how I felt.

"I remember one day out in the woods when night fell too suddenly and I was afraid. And just as suddenly, there ahead of me was my father, and without a word or question he picked me up in his arms and I felt the hard, good muscles under his shirt sleeves and nuzzled my cheek against the hair where his shirt was unbuttoned at his neck. He didn't scoff like my little friend Jessie's father did when she'd been frightened by a thunderstorm. My father saw how it was with me—by the looks of me or by my tone when I called him. I don't know. But he consoled me by saying simply that it *was* frightening to feel lost in the dark. He knew.

"I remember Christmas with his voice and Santa Claus's

11

voice matching; and the hours when nothing much happened. I just played alone with my paper dolls and read and wasn't disturbed to go and answer the phone or let in the dog. My parents felt that children, too, had a right to the 'pursuit of happiness' on their own. . . ."

In sex education—
  Love is needed
  to nourish *love*.

In contrast to Anne's case, however, there may be problems in a child's attachments to his parents which disturb his love life later. Lester, for example, was a conscientious, earnest adolescent, the son of a hard-working, silent father and a mother who was forever ill with one or another complaint. When Lester was small, he had gone to school one rainy day without his rubbers and his mother had telephoned the school to send him right home. He found her weeping. "Oh, Lester, how could you do this to me! You'll get pneumonia." And she rushed him into a hot shower and into dry clothes.

When Lester had his first date and arrived home ten minutes later than the agreed hour, he found his father trying to help his mother recover from a fainting spell. On seeing her son, she revived quickly and remonstrated, "Lester, darling, how could you? With all I do for you all the time! You had me so worried, I thought I would die."

In happier moments, his mother "adored" him. In return he adored her with one side of him. But with another he unconsciously resented her. He longed to escape from her bondage but felt "bad" because of this wish. He never leveled at her a single angry or resentful word. In fact, so instilled was he with the necessity of being grateful that he did not dare admit any contrary feelings even to himself.

At thirty-five Lester still had not married. "It's always the same between me and a woman," he confessed ruefully. "After a while I either begin doing inexplicable things like forgetting

12

dates or acting like a boor or a bore so that before I know it, I'm out on my ear."

Without knowing it, Lester was carrying over his earlier feelings, trying alternately to escape or to punish some other woman for what the first woman in his life had done. Never having learned to face or handle these feelings, he went on helplessly in their grip.

In a sense, Lester was "stuck" in his attachment to his mother. Even after her death, he kept finding her in other women, bringing her, as it were, back into his life. With every woman he still acted like a child with a mother, not like a man with a sweetheart or wife. Even though he had remained unaware of it, the anger he had felt toward his mother had grown so big that it formed a barrier against loving any woman.

Anger at moments all through life
is natural and normal.
But when it grows too big,
then it becomes chief enemy to love.

"B" IS FOR BODY SENSITIVITY   At any age people communicate their feelings for one another with their bodies. A mother, for instance, communicates tenderness in the curve of her arm and the cherishing bend of her body as she holds her infant. A father communicates protectiveness in the handclasp by which he steers his child across a busy street. The timid kiss of two adolescents brings a message of not being alone in hesitant waiting. The rhythm of body to body in the final experience of loving tells more fully of feelings than anything else.

Right from the beginning a child is equipped to feel bodily pleasure. When he is small, *the way his body reacts with sensitivity to physical contact helps him to learn that he is loved.* Body-feelings help to convey emotional attachments long before he can comprehend the meaning of words.

13

In this sense, sexual feeling starts at birth. But it is not full-fledged at birth. Nor is it sexual in the adult sense. For one thing, its specific relation to the sexual organs has to develop.

At different periods of the child's development, just as there appears to be an orderly sequence of attachments, so also does there appear to be an orderly sequence of body sensitivities. There are shifts as to which parts of the body bring the most valued body-feelings.

In brief: During infancy a child's whole body reacts with satisfaction to being touched and cuddled. He responds with a sensitivity that involves all his body surfaces. Particularly important, too, at this period is the sensitivity of mouth and lips. Both physical and emotional nourishment come to a baby as he is held, as he is fed. Through eating, through sucking, through the sensations of touch and of physical support, he receives in primitive body communications the most essential of all emotional foodstuffs, love.

Somewhat later another area of his body takes on more importance. He becomes more focused on the pleasure he has in evacuating. Not that the process has not been pleasant before. It has, as every observant parent can note by the infant's satisfied wrigglings during a bowel movement and by the way his whole little body seems to smooth out and let go of its tensions right afterward. But when he reaches the age where he becomes more aware of his movements, the body sensitivity in the organs involved seems to increase. The same happens with urination a bit later and with the parts of the body connected with this.

Then if emotional development progresses properly on its road toward sexual maturing, a child begins to notice and to focus on the genital area and to find that the pleasantest of his body sensations come from there. (Obviously this is an essential step for him to take if adult sexual satisfactions are to be reached.)

In the course of his growth, every child learns many things about his body and its sensitivities. Some of what he learns helps him in his development. Some hinders him and impedes mature adjustments.

Many young couples, married in hopefulness, find it difficult to reach mutual completion. The proportion of marriages that go on the rocks because of the resulting unhappiness is startlingly high. This is common knowledge today.

But what is not common knowledge is that behind such blocking of mature sexual enjoyment are feelings that have become disproportionate, as, for instance, fear that is inappropriate and that has grown too big.

Strangely, too great fear not only can make for sexual constriction—for frigidity, for impotence, for lack of sexual competence or receptivity in varying degrees—fear can also make for sexual splurging. One important reason why the delinquent rushes here and there in sexual exploits is to try by his prowess to disprove his fear.

Tough young Jamey, in his teens, boasts of exploits galore. Looking back, his memory runs always to how his father had threatened him as a child: "If I catch you playing with yourself again, I'll break every bone in your body! You'll ruin yourself." Then, for one reason because Jamey in his childish way had thought there was a bone in his erect penis, he had in his mind connected his father's threat to that part of his body in particular. He grew terribly afraid that in some strange fashion he had ruined himself. Both out of hostility to his father and because of an exaggerated and compulsive necessity to prove to himself that his body was still capable, he rushed headlong over and over into escapades. Consciously he denied having any fear. He was full of bravado. But the unconscious, hidden fear continued to push him into what he did. In spite of his grown-up swagger, he still felt himself a little child trying to disprove his father and his father's threat.

15

It is not only such exaggerated threats, however, that bring on too great fear. Sometimes far more considered warnings do, too. Lorna, for instance, at three, out in the garden one day, sat on the grass curled over in the lovely, lithe, loose-jointed way that small children have, examining her genitals. Her mother came quietly out of the house to hang up the clothes, caught sight of the child, recoiled and cautioned, "Keep your fingers away from there, Lorna."

Later she picked Lorna up and, cuddling her, spoke to her gently about "keeping clean" and "not ever touching." She didn't want her little girl to "make herself sore."

Many similar episodes reiterated the fear Lorna's mother had carried over from her own childhood.

And so, little Lorna grew up and married. And when her husband held her in his arms like a baby being cuddled it was welcome. "But when my husband approaches intercourse, something makes me turn away."

In Lorna the focus of body enjoyments had remained fastened to babyhood, which is the period in life when cuddling is most important. As with Mary, body sensitivity had failed to progress to where genital pleasure could come with peaceful freedom. "I guess I'm not normal," Lorna would say, "but I simply don't have impulses of that sort." Actually her impulses were perfectly normal. Her sexual-emotional development, however, had been arrested through fear that had grown too big.

When childish fears grow out of proportion they can *anesthetize normal sensations* and keep mature sexual satisfactions from being reached.

Too great and crippling fears may be touched off also because of the overwhelming quality of the sexual feelings themselves.

Sexual feelings are big feelings. They are strong feelings. They carry the person along in their surge. As we shall see, particularly at certain times in his existence, the child may be

16

frightened by the internal vehemence of them. We recognize this in the young adolescent, remembering it perhaps in ourselves. The tremendous urge for contact, the sense of danger, the pulling back.

And sometimes the pulling back remains after marriage.

This happens, for one thing, if a child comes to feel, as Mary and Jamey and Lorna did, that body-feelings are "bad." Nothing may be said about being hurt. But still a child seems to figure that if his body is "bad" in having pleasure, it might be hurt to punish him as he deserves. Or, even worse, that the person who lives in the body might be rejected or hurt.

In any event, there are so many hazards to healthy maturing that children need us greatly to help them safeguard and fortify the conviction that the bodily sensitivity granted to human beings can be a thing of beauty, dignity, and grace.

"C" IS FOR   One's concept of a subject is the general no-
CONCEPTS   tion or idea one has of that subject. Mary, after childbirth, had an idea that all her insides would fall out when she got out of bed. In spite of the reassurance she had from the doctor that she was all right, she had almost fainted from fear. Tom had an idea that demonstrativeness was not for married people. Mary had told him otherwise and the doctor had added the fact that affection to a wife during pregnancy was particularly important. Tom knew what was what. And yet, he could not express affection. Something had gotten in his way.

At this point, neither Mary nor Tom lacked real facts. They had been given the needed information. And yet, even though this could register as "what-I-know," it still did not carry over usably into "what-I-live-by." Fact and imaginings had mingled. And imaginings won.

A child hears, sees, smells, feels, and senses many things, and these he puts together in his own fashion. Not infrequently he transforms them in ways that to adult logic seem silly, improbable, or impossible. He expands them often beyond all reason, and twines them together into unrealistic shapes. Strange as it may seem, *many of the failures in adult sex living are due to holdovers from the childish imaginings that ran through earlier days.*

To cite a case in point: Ned during his first three years had slept with his parents in their apartment's one bedroom. Many times after they believed him to be asleep, he would hear sounds and would awaken from half-dreaming to sudden wide-eyed horror. What he half saw in the dark he transformed with his mind to make his own meanings: His mother, his darling mother, was being hurt—maybe killed. For years this lay forgotten. Obviously he came to know better. In fact, his father in fatherly fashion gave him all the "facts of life." But still, in his marriage, sex was troubled. He was "too fast," too precipitous. "I know," he said, "it's no good."

But not until the veil over memories lifted during psychotherapy did he realize that a big part of his difficulty was caused by fear. Not fear of the actual but fear of what he had imagined. In his mind, he had carried this—hidden—into his marriage. Each time he started his love-making successfully, the thought would come cutting through him like the swift shiver of a knife: He might hurt his wife! He might kill her! And then his power to sustain his excitement would leave.

There are many feelings related to the child's attachments that he embroiders with his imaginings. There are many feelings about his body and his body sensations that he embroils with unreal concerns.

And often—

> *A child's imaginings seem so real to him that he takes them as factual.* They then shape his sex life more than the facts that we bring.

"It's so strange," says Fran's mother. "I keep telling her things again and again and yet she never seems to have heard them before. You wonder what she has in her head to keep her ears stopped up against what I say."

Fran's mother sensed that something was keeping Fran from hearing. But she did not realize that it was Fran's own fictions which were making so much noise of their own in Fran's head that they drowned out the factual explanations. A child's concepts about sex grow from many sources. From what he sees and hears, from his sensations—from a multitude of experiences and from how he takes these. From his daydreams and imaginings and from how we receive them. And, finally, from the facts we impart.

A child still needs our facts. They should be frank and simple and within his reach—not over his head when he is little and not belittling his comprehension when he is bigger. How to tell him the facts as well as what to tell him calls for thoughtful consideration. All this we shall come to as we go on.

Meanwhile—

Let's not slide back into the old way of thinking that unless we're focusing on how to answer a child's questions, we're not talking about sex education. . . .

For—

In order to help our children gain a vital kind of sex education to live by, *we must consider many more things than how to tell about sex.*

Above all, we need to remember—

In sound SEX EDUCATION
FEELINGS come FIRST.

PART 2 | PLANNING PRACTICAL STEPS

3 | Growing Up Is More Than Growing Older

"My father," says Cathy, "is such a baby. He's always asking my mother what he should do. And when she gets cross
with him, he looks so innocent. He never, never did anything
he shouldn't! He acts like a lamb or like a child who's too scared

Father: "Mother! Mother! Where's my sweater?"
Junior, disgustedly: "She's not your mother. She's your Nora;
   or your wife."

to stand up for itself. Outside he's so big but inside he's so little."

Later Cathy adds, "He has to say 'yes' to everything. He gets all mixed up that his wife's his Mommie. I think he's just the chicken-pecked man!"

The hen-pecked man, the baby doll, the frigid wife, the impotent husband, the homosexual, the gallant bachelor, the man or woman who marries and divorces repeatedly—all are people who stopped in their growing up.

One can grow in body. One can grow in mind. But one can, at the same time, fail to grow up emotionally. As one brilliant engineer said, "When I was in high school I was mathematically mature; but as a husband I'm still sexually a child."

Sexual maturing and emotional maturing are indissolubly geared together. And so a major task in sex education is knowing how to help our children progress in emotionally healthy fashion.

Satisfactions Needed for Sexual Maturing

Just as physical health demands that certain nutritional values be had all through life, so also does sexual-emotional health demand that there be certain emotional foodstuffs.

A child needs *love* above all else.

We give our love by holding a child very close when he is little. By letting him, when he is ready, walk step by step on his own. By not clinging to him. By not pressing him. By appreciating the achievements of which he is capable, knowing that for him *achievement* and *appreciation* are both necessary emotional foods if he is to mature. We are glad when we see his own selfhood and self-confidence grow.

We give love by helping a child feel that *sense of belonging* and of being wanted that all human beings need deeply. By letting him know that it is not just the "nice" half of him that we want, but that we can accept every kind of feeling in him; that he can share himself with us as he really is.

Giving this sort of *understanding* and *acceptance* is far from easy.

When a child is full of unreasonable wishes and demands, when he seems absurdly or irrationally "scarey" or when his anger dashes into the picture, our acceptance is apt to crumble and scatter to the winds. This naturally happens some of the time. But when it happens most of the time or all of the time, it makes a child believe that he should only show his "good" and "nice" feelings. It makes him fear that he might not be wanted if he dared to share the painful feelings which he needs most to share. And this can spread into his sex life. As a perfectly "good" adolescent put it, "If my girl finds out how bad I am underneath, she'd never look at me again. And so I only show her a part of myself. It's like living on a powder keg. You're so anxious that if you let go anywhere, something you don't want seen may slip out. So you stay all huddled up inside yourself and feel terribly lonely." Capacity for the true intimacy called for in sex relations is lost.

As part of his sex education—

A child needs love that lets him find in his day-by-day living *that he does not have to shove any kind of feeling off into hiding.*

We show our love truly when we can learn, at least some of the time, to meet the kind of feelings that are commonly called "undesirable" with sincere acceptance. As if we were saying with our own feelings: "I, too, have felt that way and I know how it is." This does not mean, however, that we show love by permitting license. Quite the contrary. We show love by firmly guiding a child into learning sound ways of control. (This will become clearer a bit farther on.)

We give our love also in a way most vital for a child's sex

education when we can accept in our children that propulsive strong drive common to every human being for the unashamed *joy of having good body-feelings* in a variety of ways all through life.

"It's so wonderful to spread your chest and take a deep breath and laugh in the wind," says a ten-year-old.

"It's so wonderful to feel those thousand little lightning whispers that curl all through you when you're kissed," says a girl of seventeen.

As part of his sex education—

A child needs love that helps him know surely
that *good sensations will* not *hurt*
his body.

The urge to feel that one's body is as whole and sound as it can be is a vital and important human wish. Strange though it may seem to adults, many children are particularly anxious about their reproductive organs. They imagine often that handicaps or hurts from other parts of the body can settle here.

"Can I ever have a baby?" a little deaf girl asked wistfully.

"Why, darling?"

"Because—because maybe," with hands clutching her stomach, "maybe my inside me won't be able to hear that I want one." She feared that the handicap to her ears had jumped to where her babies would grow.

Similarly, many a child fears that a skinned knee, a vaccination, a bloody nose can somehow spread or run to the genitals and bring permanent injury there. It is wise, therefore, as we've already gathered, never needlessly to level at a child the slightest threat to the genitals themselves.

A child's satisfactions, necessary for healthy sexual progress, come basically through his relationships or attachments within his family—most of all through what his mother and father are to him. Through them he gets his most important messages of

26

love, of appreciation, of being wanted and so of belonging. They encourage his achievements. They react to his pleasurable body-feelings and to the aches and pains and hurts his body encounters. They may try to give him whatever he wants. But they can never give him all.

Those Inevitable Frustrations

No matter how we may try to let our children have the satisfactions they need for sexual-emotional maturing, there are frustrations that come as surely as the clouds and the wind and the rain.

There are those frustrations over which none of us has any control.

No person alive can move through life escaping them altogether. Nor is any age without its own brand. To the small infant who is physically hungry, the brief wait for a blouse to be unbuttoned or a bottle to be heated brings frustration. When teething is painful, this spells frustration—frustration to the urge for the bodily comfort and pleasure on which sexual fulfillment depends. The same is true when a common cold takes over, when a stool is hard and painful, or when any of the hundred and one ills that descend on most growing children come.

Anyone could continue enumerating things that bring other sorts of frustration: the frustration to a small child's need for concretely expressed love, for instance, that comes when Mother is sick or goes to the hospital to have a new baby so that physical closeness and proximity are temporarily lost. The frustration to his sense of belonging when a child must leave home every morning before he feels at home in his school.

There are times in almost every life when one is realistically hungry—for food, for rest, for comfort, for beauty, for accomplishment, for belonging, companionship, and appreciation—for understanding which comes sympathetically or for freedom from pain.

But in addition, *all the time that a child is growing there are frustrations because of wishes inside that cannot be realized.*

"I wish," says a small boy wistfully, "I wish I could take home a mother who would be my always-good-feeding mommy and my always-good-dog."

He is wishing for the imagined yet impossible perfection of being cared for by a dream mother great enough to allay every hunger who would serve him with the unflagging obedience of a faithful dog.

Some wishes are appropriate and healthy and call for the fullest satisfactions that can be had. In contrast, some wishes are not suitable or appropriate for a child to have granted at his age.

As an example, twelve-year-old Ethel, a fast-maturing and idealistic youngster, had a terrific crush on an eighteen-year-old neighbor boy. Inside her ran all the thrills of budding sexuality. She fantasied his creeping into her room stealthily and overpowering her. Although this is a common wish at her age, if it had actually happened every sex act to Ethel after that could have spelled not only "rape" but something filled with secret horror. Much as she desired warm enjoyment, a pattern of frigidity would have been set. She would have become afraid to move forward, afraid of what lay ahead.

Frustration was painful, but less painful than the alternative.

Obviously *what is nourishing at one time of life can cause indigestion at another.* Being fed chunks of meat is not an appropriate way for a newborn to have its protein needs taken care of. Mama-cuddling is not an appropriate way for the adolescent to get his love needs supplied. Nor would the carrying out of Ethel's wish have been an appropriate way for sexual satisfactions to be gained by a twelve-year-old.

At each stage there are sound and appropriate means through

which a child obtains the basic satisfactions he needs for his sexual-emotional progress. (We'll look at these in connection with the various developmental periods as we take them up.) What is important to see now is that—

A wish APPROPRIATELY MET
LEADS best
to the NEXT STEPS
in sexual maturing.

Developmentally, a baby has the least tolerance for frustration. In general, tolerance increases with age although it varies in different individuals and in the same individual at different times. To gain increasing tolerance for frustration is essential as one grows. Otherwise one stumbles or falls too painfully when one encounters the frustrations that are bound to come. Tolerance, however, develops most soundly if it is not too much taxed in the early years.

Sometimes the pain of frustration may be lessened by helping the child to gain a more *appropriate satisfaction*.

Two-year-old Jane, for instance, watches her mother breast-feeding two-month-old Nora. Shyly Jane edges over. And suddenly the tears well up.

"Mommy, Mommy," she sobs, her pain very vivid. "Oh, Mommy, I want some too."

"I know, darling," says her mother with sympathy and understanding. "I know you'd like me to be feeding you this way. . . ."

She pauses to hear if Jane wants to say more. "I wanna come up," Jane mutters. "I wanna suck."

"You wish you could suck like the baby does and like you used to. But you can't any more, honey."

Jane glowers resentfuly. "You're bad. I don't like you."

"I know, it makes you feel mad at Mommy. In a little while,

though, you can come up in my lap. And we'll see what we can do."

Then, after she has finished breast-feeding the baby, Mommy fetches a bottle and fills it with the chocolate milk which she knows Jane likes. And she holds Jane in her lap and lets her suck.

Sometimes, when a child has missed certain satisfactions that he should have had at one stage, we can help him make up for these later in appropriate ways. Jane's mother happened also to be doing this. Having weaned Jane too early, she was belatedly making up now for what Jane had missed.

In addition, she realized that even though this might lessen the pain, some frustration was still present. And she knew, as all of us need to know, that—

Frustration always brings anger, hostility,
bitterness, or
resentment, call it what one will.
This is normal and natural.

It's normal at times to have wishes that cannot be granted. Normal to be angry at times. Normal to be afraid, too, at times. And at times to feel "bad" or guilty.

What we need to remember is that difficulties enter in sex and loving when such feelings accumulate and grow too big.
Therefore—

**A key problem in sex education is to see that
feelings which interfere with sex and loving
DO NOT PILE UP INSIDE.**

Anger is especially crucial in this whole matter. For, whenever we are disappointed, in pain, hurt, frightened, anxious, or wanting, whenever life falls short of even impossible expectations, whenever we must wait till later for what we long for now —anger enters. But despite its frequent, normal presence, we have been taught to deny it. Anger toward parents most of all.

30

And yet, anger toward parents is the most natural and normal of all childish angers.

Parents are human. They have their own problems. Their behavior with their children cannot be ideal. Even when they live up to the fullest in being "good parents," they must be the chief deniers of the child's inappropriate wishes. For this is part of being good parents.

Parents have to stand as authority, as the power that must often refuse what a child wants or enforce what he doesn't want. This is their job. And so, their child inevitably resents them at moments throughout his childhood.

In addition, their child has inside him holdovers from the earliest years.

When he is little, he feels that his mother and father are all-powerful. These two big people bring him everything he has. Just as Mother brings him his bottle, so he imagines she brings him his toothache. Just as Father brings him a ride in the car, so he takes Mother away for dinner. Mother and Father are the child's greatest heroes. They are also his greatest villains. And so his biggest wishes and his biggest angers naturally go toward them.

But this anger above all he is taught not to express.

In consequence, *it is this very anger toward parents that stays most frequently hidden inside*. There it accumulates. Grows too big. Spreads to other people. Blocks sexual progress. (This we have seen.)

When a child is well loved, he has more security with which to handle frustration and the angry feelings that frustration brings. But where anger has mounted too high, it can even keep him from accepting the love that he needs.

We need to help a child *keep normal anger normal*. And this means getting it out into the open—the anger to his parents most of all.

For it is true—

**LOVE grows most soundly
when ANGER
IS NOT DENIED.**

More broadly, what we have been saying is that—

It's important for us to see that our children *take in many
hearty satisfactions* if they are to mature sexually.

But that is not all.

We must also help them learn to *let out* those *feelings*
which, if stored up, can become so big they poison intimacy and love.

Controls Are Essential

A father writes: "We parents today are in a real predicament.
We hear so much about the dangers of feelings being held in.
And yet, we know it's dangerous too for feelings to splash out
indiscriminately. We can't tolerate the idea of having our children run riot. What can we do?"

He has put very clearly a question that concerns us all in
sex education.

One thing that can help is for us to recognize that *feeling and
doing are two different matters.* If we can keep this difference
clear in our own minds, we won't have so much difficulty helping our children get it clear in theirs.

Accepting how a child feels does not mean that we accept
his giving in to impulses willy-nilly.

A child needs our *firm understanding of feelings.*

But he also needs our *firm stand on actions.*

This *combination* gives him the security to develop his
own firmness and self-control.

Control comes best when a person learns as a child that feelings and acts call for different treatment.

FEELINGS must be helped to
COME OUT HONESTLY
for what they are.

ACTS need often to be
HELD BACK
and
CURTAILED.

Fifteen-year-old Mona sputters, "I wish I could go to the movies with Johnny this evening. Oh, I wish, I wish I could."

"I know you want to." Sympathetically Mona's mother acknowledges and accepts the wishful feeling. "But not on a school night!" curtails the act.

How "Manage" Feelings?

Telling a child he should not feel what he feels or want what he wants does no good. We, as adults, know how this is. "I shouldn't want to nibble between meals" does not make the dieting easier. "I shouldn't want a cigarette" doesn't make the desire go away. Nor does saying "You shouldn't want sexual intercourse before you're married" make the adolescent's urge disappear. In fact, this kind of adamant attitude, this ignoring of the pain of the wanting, this by-passing of sensitive feelings and of the ache of not having only makes matters worse.

Calling the feeling by a sweeter name does no good either.

"Go 'way! Go 'way!" small Joe pushes his father and, with tears in his eyes, he rushes onto his mother's lap. He wants to be the "onliest" in Mother's life, the normal wish of a child of his age, and he is momentarily resentful of his father for standing in his way.

"Poor darling," says his mother. She picks him up and cuddles him. "He's so tired!"

By explaining away his feelings under cover of "tiredness"

33

she is teaching him that he should use subterfuge and that the real feelings should be by-passed and denied. How, then, will he ever learn to manage their expression? How can one learn to steer sexual wishes if one denies that the wishes are there? How can one cut down the anger or fear that interferes with loving if one denies that they exist?

With these questions in mind, let's go on to another scene.

An adorable two-year-old sits in her stroller. As Father pushes her through the supermart she wants grapes, cookies, potato chips, suckers. "One sucker, that's all, Bettina," says Father.

"No," shrieks Bettina, "I want more." And she throws the sucker onto the floor. "More!" her voice rises. "I want more. More. More."

"You want more and more," says the grocery boy, passing. He has a chuckle in his voice and a note running under it that says, "I know how that feels." "But," he adds out loud, "hold your horses, baby. Daddy said 'No!' "

Bettina stares. Stops shrieking, mouth spreading into a grin.

Inadvertently the boy had done just the right things. He had acknowledged how Bettina felt. He had named her feelings with a sense of kinship as a part of being alive. (Who doesn't wish for more?) And then he had stated how Bettina needed realistically to act.

One handles feelings best by meeting them squarely. Part of sex education lies in helping our children say feelings out straight.

> *Identify feelings for what they are.* This is your first important step.

When feelings are already out in the open, as Bettina's were, then the naming of the feeling along with the giving of understanding can of itself be enough. Oftener a child needs to bring feelings out further. But along channels or pathways that are physically, socially, and morally acceptable. *Identify proper channels*. This is your second step.

"You feel this way. That makes you *wish* to do lots of things you cannot do actually. You *want* to do those things. You can draw or paint out what you'd like to do, or write it out for me in a story, or play it out with your dolls or your toy soldiers. Or talk it out to me." (These are safe channels.) "But so far as doing what's expected, you have to act the right way all the same."

This directing of action into safe channels reduces the intensity of the aching feelings. The sharing with you reduces the intensity of the child's fear that he may run amuck. It gives you a chance to help him know that he can depend on you to teach him how to control his acts.

Because our children by and large have not been taught how to manage feelings, this needs to be defined for them again and again. From Mother or Father: "We used to think you shouldn't say anything about wanting things you couldn't possibly have or wanting to do things you couldn't possibly do. We thought it most important of all not to talk about feelings of being jealous or resentful or angry or chip-on-the-shoulderish. But we've learned better. We know now it's best to talk about any and all feelings. Fears also. Better to share them out loud."

"You feel this way. . . . You wish to do lots of things you really can't do. . . ." opens the door to telling more. It helps share what one fancies, what one "would like to do but can't."

When a child wants something, help him say it out.

He can't always have what he wants.

But—*when he talks about it and we accept his feelings, we feed him* UNDERSTANDING. *And this, in essence, communicates love.*

Then the third step is called for, particularly when angry

feelings are involved. It has to do with what, or rather with whom, one feels angry—with the object or target of one's anger. We need to *identify the object*. This is the point.

"You'd like to do lots of things you can't do . . . to whom?" Barbara does to Bobby. Bobby is the immediate, short-range object. But Barbara also feels resentment toward Mother for having to give time and attention to Bobby and for being generally crotchety with her. And Barbara feels resentment to Father also for his Bobby-doting air. These feelings join with many past resentments that have piled up. Barbara's parents are the long-range, original objects of her wrath. (Just as every child's parents normally are.)

Finally, however, Barbara manages to say straightforwardly to her mother, "You should learn to take a little patience in your head. I think you're a little too harsh on me. These days you don't have any sweet in you. It's all ruined up and spoils all my fun. You've been so ornery it's hard to stay in the same house. I think you've got a whole blab of mad in your head and need to get it out some other way, not on me."

Ask yourself: Would I be shocked if a child of mine spoke to me this way? Would I say, "Stop it. That's disrespectful." Or could I hear him out and consider it healthy and fine that he has courage enough and confidence enough in me to tell this to me directly? Could I realize that this is better than if he were to hammer now at another child, or later at a marriage partner in blind attempts to get back at me?

Barbara's mother did listen to Barbara. She nodded. "I don't wonder that you've been angry at me. I've been mighty difficult."

"Oh," said Barbara with quick warmth flowing, "that's all right, Mother. Everybody gets mad at times."

"Often, often, especially at their parents. All children do." Repeat this to your youngsters so they know that you know how they are bound to feel at times and that you don't think them monsters for it. "All children imagine all sorts of things they'd like to do to their parents when they're angry—things they cannot really do. . . ."

"Why don't you draw some," suggests nine-year-old Rod's father.

So Rod gets out his crayons and draws an enormous meat grinder grinding up a figure labeled "mean mother," with the boy who is running the machine labeled "Rod." And at his other side a great sink with an opening marked "Garbage disposal all ready for Dad."

This is one of the *hows* by which feelings can be channeled into acts.

There are *times* and *places,* of course—the *whens* and the *wheres* in which such feelings may be expressed. Not when guests are visiting; not when one is on a crowded elevator; not when Mother is in the critical stages of baking a cake. In private. Just as with other intimate matters.

Even so, it is often easier for parents to have a child kick at them than to say, "I hate you." The kicking can be excused more readily as "childish." "I hate you" is much harder to bear.

But this is very important: It does a child absolutely no good to get out his feelings in physical attacks on his parents. It does him no good to get them out in actual destructiveness either. It does no more good when he is little for him to punch his father or hit his mother than it does later for him to steal cars or to run wild sexually, unconsciously hitting at his parents by doing what will hurt them.

Our eventual goal, so far as sex education is concerned, is for the child to learn gradually to get things straightforwardly off his chest so that when he has grown he will be able to clear the air honestly every so often of the tensions that normally arise between married people.

Letting out along safe channels all through the years; *discovering securely that love can be regained after the un-*

loving moments are passed—this makes it more possible for a child to shed the feelings that interfere with later sex life.

It prevents such feelings from piling up and causing him to function in immature ways.

Kathy has typed:
> Once upon a time there was a mother mokey. And her little mokeys names were Nip mip and pip. One day mother mokey was going to have another baby. By and by she did. She was very happy and the little mokeys were very VERY JELLOS becas the baby mokey got all the ATENCHON in the house.

Mother thinks:
> That's a good way to channel out those feelings. Now they won't be stored inside to come out later on an undeserving spouse.

We need to remind ourselves that even though a person has long since forgotten what happened in childhood, he can still continue on in a grown body with an infant's or little child's feelings at the steering wheel.

This happened with Lisa, a young married woman. When she was seven her mother became seriously ill and, without adequate explanation, Lisa was bundled off to boarding school.

This made her feel unloved and unwanted as had other things earlier which, in their ignorance, her parents had done or not done. In her mind, Lisa wanted to bite and crush them both. Her jaws, she pictured, were like a nutcracker that would do the crushing by coming together and tightening hard. In adulthood, her sexual adjustment was very difficult. All unconsciously, she had transferred the nutcracker fantasy to another opening in her body. In intercourse she could not have a complete orgasm. For in orgasm the vaginal walls contract, and whenever she felt these contractions beginning she would suddenly lose all excitement. Behind this lay the immature fear of doing with this other part of her body what she had fantasied and feared doing with her mouth as a child. Behind it lay further fear of the retaliation she had envisioned might be done her.

In short: When someone big and trustworthy can hold your hand and say, "Yes, these are your feelings. You do want more," or "You do feel mighty angry . . . or scared" (identifying and naming whatever feelings one sees or hears), then a load is lifted. It lifts even more if the child can talk on and on, airing imaginings and all. But at one and the same time, a child needs to know that what he actually *does* must be *controlled*. Only then can he feel safe in growing up.

4 | Fact and Fiction in Sex Education

We have learned in sex education not to hand a child fiction for truth as we did formally in such stories as that of the stork or of babies being brought in the doctor's little black bag or growing in the shining cups of flowers. But what we have not had sufficient chance of learning is that the child often hands himself his own fiction.

His Fantastic Ideas Are Real to Him

In any sex information we bring to a child, we are apt to bump up against his own imaginings.

Steven asked his mother, "Where do babies grow?" And she explained, "Inside the mother in a special place."

"Oh," he answered with wide eyes, "the baby's right next to the toast."

"In the mommy's eating stomach," he elaborated later.

"Oh no, darling," his mother quickly explained. "The baby grows in a special place inside the mother called the uterus." Nor did she give any further thought to what was on Steven's mind, she was so bent on furnishing facts.

This is what many of us have thought we should do in sex education. We jump in with scientific information and, without meaning to, disregard what the child is thinking.

40

We usually believe that we help feelings straighten out best by furnishing facts first.

The opposite is true. *We help facts straighten out best by attending to feelings and imaginings first.*

By bringing in answers too fast, we say in effect, without intending to, "Keep your feelings and imaginings to yourself."

And this is not good.

What young Hank says is pertinent. "When I keep my thoughts to myself," he murmurs, "nobody has a chance to convince me of anything else."

The result is that we leave a child in his immaturity to handle unfounded feelings, false ideas, and faulty interpretations alone.

Hidden They Grow

Sensing that adults will fail to understand their strange creations, children often give lip service to the facts we offer. But their own fiction still rules in their heads. It colors what they live by with all the more intensity when it has become a secret that must be guarded.

Childish IMAGININGS frequently
INFLUENCE
SEXUAL ATTITUDES
far more than FACTS.

Marnie's story shows how childish imaginings may grow beyond reason's control.

When Marnie's mother was going to have a new baby, she carefully gave Marnie concrete information about the wonderful event ahead. She had Marnie help her fix up the new crib, the new room, the new diapers. However, in the fashion of a three-year-old still very attached to her mother, Marnie wished with desperation to keep her mother all to herself. She clung and hung onto her. She cried when her mother went out.

41

"What makes you so naughty?" her mother chided, and Marnie caught the irritation in her voice. Much as Marnie yearned for the comfort of sharing her wishes, she dared not. In her mind, their greediness made her too "bad." And into her crept a bewildered and aching sense of defeat.

Then anger curled around in great swirls inside her. And to herself Marnie made up fantastic stories about what, in her anger, she wanted to do.

"I'll chop her!" Marnie muttered. "I'll chop her all up." And then, stumbling over a rock she whimpered, "Marnie got hurt 'cause she's a bad girl."

Moreover, as if to find comfort in body pleasure, Marnie went back to what she had done when she was a baby. She went back to sucking her thumb.

Her mother looked at her and sighed, "Oh, dear." And her mother put on a breaking-her-of-the-nasty-habit campaign. Marnie tried to cooperate. She would slap her own hand, "You're a bad Marnie." She would cry. She would try. She would suck again.

And then one night Marnie woke and her mother was gone. Marnie took her absence as desertion. She imagined her mother had left her to punish her for being "bad." This Marnie did in spite of the facts that had been supplied.

Years later Marnie, grown into a woman, found marriage haunted with vague and unfounded fears that if she got pregnant she would be deserted. In her unconscious, pregnancy and desertion were knotted together. This came between her and her husband, who wanted children very much. The childish fancies Marnie had originally connected with a baby's arrival had become entangled in her mind. She interpreted falsely that her intense wish for an exclusive love attachment to Mother, her anger, and her comforting body-feelings, all made her "awful." She mistakenly explained her mother's absence as pun-

42

ishment due her. Her fantasies then had been hidden and lost. But their power and influence remained.

Her feelings and the stories which they prompted her to make up had drowned out the story she had heard from her mother about the wonders of birth.

At each stage of development a child is apt to have certain sorts of imaginings in his head. Nor is this strange. The youth approaching manhood, for instance, senses the sexual stirrings of maturity. His daydreams are full of wishes about finding his particular girl.

Because we know that such adolescent daydreams are normal, we meet them sympathetically. We can do the same with the less familiar, stranger imaginings that are typical during younger years as we come to recognize these.

In general, a child's fantasies about sex are connected with the *personal attachments most valued by him* and with *the portions of his body that concern him most at his particular level of development*. When he is at the toilet-training stage, for instance, many of his fantasies have to do with his attachment to the person who devotes time to his training and with the products of his body and the feelings he has about them. (See Chapter 8.)

He wishes many things. His wishes take his imagination flying into daydreams, or wish-fantasies, about "what I'd like to have." When what is longed for is not forthcoming, his angry feelings make him "want to do something with his mads." Anger-fantasies enter about "what mean things I'd like to do." Fear-fantasies rise also with imaginings about "what I'm afraid might happen to me." Left in the dark, all of these become bigger and more frightening.

And so we can see how poignantly children need us to heed their fantasies and the feelings from which the fantasies spring.

43

But, up until recent years, we were handicapped. We did not have sufficient knowledge about the imaginings of children to take them into account. A large portion of the failures in sex education were in fact due to this omission.

Today we can do better.

Out of the psychological work of recent years, countless things we did not know about children's imaginings have come to light.

But still it's hard. There are innumerable childish fantasies that seem bizarre and strange. Perhaps we recoil, "Oh no! That's abnormal! My child never felt that way." Perhaps we react with wonder and doubting, "How can this be?"

However, many of us who are parents and teachers today are still able to say, "Even though this sounds unbelievable, as I go on it may become clearer." Many of us want to be more sensitively in touch with what children really are like.

And we know: The mere fact that a child's thoughts are unspoken does not mean they are not present.

Some of every child's fantasies go into his unconscious and become embedded there. When sexual problems arise they are often due to these forgotten thoughts. Probing for what has been lost, however, is dangerous business. It is something that only an experienced psychotherapist should do. Not parents or teachers.

In contrast there are those fantasies that stand at the threshold of children's minds, ready to come out if they are given opportunities. These need not get buried too deeply and grow out of proportion. When they are moved into the light and are safely shared, they are seen more clearly for what they are. Then we can help our children set them straight.

As we gain insight into what is natural for children to feel and fantasy, we won't make the mistake of believing them silly or "bad" for having such thoughts. We won't disregard or bypass what our children long so poignantly to share. We will receive their own stories with more sympathetic welcome when these start to poke their heads out through the door.

Perhaps this is all a child needs. For, when he can read acceptance in our faces, he may spontaneously carry his thoughts into the open, seeking the release and relief that sharing brings.

So it was with Laura, whose adoration of her doctor-father knew no bounds. One night she sat watching her pretty brown-haired mother dress for a dance. Nodding her scraggly red head every so often and punctuating her remarks with a smile that showed the two empty spaces in her mouth, Laura rambled on dreamily with childish admiration for her mother mingled with envious wishes. "When I grow up," she sighed, looking her mother up and down, "I'm going to be even prettier. Red hair's what I think Daddy likes best. And when I grow up I'll go to lots more dances. And *my* husband, too, will be a doctor. And I'll look even more beautiful in *my* green formula. . . ."

Her mother smiled sympathetically. Inside she chortled, "She's obnoxious but normal, bless her." She knew that such daydreams are part of the stuff of which marriage is made. "If she gets in too deep, I can haul her out better after having heard what's on her mind. And I know, too, that after she raves on enough, she'll be readier to hear what I say!"

But, we ask, how about children when they're not as free as Laura in tumbling things out? What about it when a child doesn't talk?

This same question applies to children's unspoken questions about sex. In fact, a child's unasked questions have usually gotten tied up inside him because of his fantasies—of imagined "badness," for instance. As if he were thinking, "I'm bad to be interested in this."

45

One of the puzzling questions in sex education is whether or not to wait for a child to talk or ask questions.

Perhaps, like Mary, each of us can remember questions we did not dare bring out. About things that worried us. . . . About things we were ashamed to talk of. . . . Afraid that if we let on that we were interested in such matters our parents might punish us or would not love us any more.

We can save our children many unwarranted worries if we help them bring their questions into the light. But, we ask, how can we detect it when a child is asking questions within himself, essentially wanting some understanding grown-up to help straighten them out?

Actually this is not too mysterious or strange a business. To do it, we need only apply in sex education what we already do automatically in many other situations.

Take our dog, for instance, when he goes to the door. What do his actions mean? What is he asking?

Take small Tommy when he looks over the arm of his highchair at the rattle that has fallen to the floor. What does he mean? What is he asking?

By thoughtful observing, we can gather, too, what Nell means when she stares at her naked little brother night and morning and in between spends much of her play holding a stick or stone or twig straight out in front of her at her crotch. (We can get it more distinctly, of course, if we know what fantasies and wonderings are frequent at Nell's age.)

Children ASK about sex
in MORE WAYS
than with
WORDS.

The language of feelings and fantasies is a strange language. The child speaks it often, as Nell did, with his movements and gestures and with his play, instead of with his tongue. When we have been initiated into some of the important fantasies at this or that stage, we can frequently get a child's meaning whatever way he indicates it. Our knowledge of the general language of fantasy-at-this-stage gives us more ability to understand a child's individual use of it and the questions he asks without words.

To Fido waiting at the door we say, "Okay, you want out!" putting his wordless question into words. "Yes," we say to Tommy, "you want Mommy to pick up your rattle."

Applying this to sex education, we can similarly say to Nell when she looks at Brother, "You're wondering what this is?"

If we know about the normal fantasies that are normally in a child's mind around this age, the sexual-emotional meaning of Nell's play becomes more apparent and we can add, "Maybe you wish you had one too?"

Some wonderings and fantasies are so nearly universal that we can count on their presence whether any evidence appears or not. If a child doesn't ask, for instance, about where he came from before he is five or so, we can surmise that he still has the question in mind. "I think maybe you wonder sometimes about when you were a little tiny baby and about where you came from" can then start him off.

When a child does not put his questions or wonderings into words, you can sometimes:

Open it up for him.

Try it by *wondering out loud* what you think he is wanting to say.

Then *wait*.

Instead of bringing in answers too swiftly *give him plenty of time*

> to put it into his own words
> and to talk on about
> what he wonders and thinks.

Perhaps then he picks up whatever feelings of his you've identified. Perhaps he doesn't.

You've said hopefully, "You're wondering. . . ." or "You want to know . . . ," believing that because of what you've just read you've gotten a kind of magic formula. "But," to quote one hopeful woman, "your surprised or coy or scared little character just says 'No' and clams up. What then? Is Mother a failure? Is the child abnormal? Or is what you've read utterly worthless?"

None of these things.

However, children don't always take to new food immediately. Nor adults either. We all know that. And having our children share their feelings and fantasies is usually new for most of us.

It takes a lot of patience. A lot of trying. And a lot of checking on one's own feelings too.

Above all—

> *Don't say you feel one way if you feel another.*
> Don't try to seem acceptant of a child's ideas if you feel unacceptant.
> You only confuse a child if you are insincere or untrue to yourself.

However, don't discard the matter either. Turn back and read over pages and passages that have seemed hard to get. Or read further and turn back later. Perhaps then, gradually or all of a sudden, what has been vague or puzzling may begin to make sense.

To Open the Door

The handling of this matter of children's questions shows us how we can approach the handling of unspoken fantasies on the whole. In fact, when a child gets used to bringing out his various wishes, angers, and fears and some of the imaginings connected with them, he will naturally bring out more of those directly connected with sex.

"You'd like to have lots of things. . . ." "You'd like to do lots of things. . . ." serve as keys to unlock the doors. But, in order for a child to feel that it's safe to step over the threshold, we need to keep pointing to safely fenced pathways along which his monsters may walk. And we need to make it very clear that those monsters may not run wild all over the place. (This we saw in the last chapter. But it does us good to recall it again and again.) To Jane who has wanted to nurse like her little brother, "You can tell me all about it." (This is a safe way for you to bring out wish-fantasies.) "And you can suck at the bottle." (That's an appropriate kind of road for those wishes to take at your age.) "But not at my breast any more." (This puts up safe limits.) . . . Or to Joe who is pushing Daddy, "You wish you could shove Daddy away. You can say so all right. Or you can pretend by pushing your daddy doll. But you can't really get rid of Daddy. He belongs right here." *The more a child can feel your sympathetic willingness to hear him out going hand in hand with your firm resolve not to let him act out indiscriminately, the safer will he feel in showing you what lies inside his mind.*

Even though he may give no word or answer, the mere fact that you have spoken with real acceptance can start him knowing, "I'm not so bad for having such feelings and thoughts."

Over and Over

One boy said, "When you've heard enough of my stories, then I'll hear yours." And "enough" means over and over.

Bringing in opportunities for feelings and imaginings to come out just once doesn't do it. Once is never enough. We need to offer opportunities repeatedly. Many, many times. The pain of the wish that cannot be fulfilled, the push of the anger and the paralysis of fear wear themselves thin and become absorbed best as they come out again and again.

Then they no longer stand in the way of a child's looking at sex facts. He is ready to compare "what's for real" with "what's pretend" and to learn with assurance which is which. (Later we'll come to more details on how such comparing can be done.)

5 | Sex Education Calls for Honesty from Adults

Most of us have picked up certain catchwords that are supposed to describe "good" sex education and these often make for confusion.

We hear: "You have to have peace and harmony in your home—both with your children and in your marriage."

We hear: "Your own attitudes toward sex must be right."

We hear: "You have to feel comfortable and easy in what you say if you say anything about sex."

Actually few of us have been brought up in a way that enables us to be altogether free and easy. Sex entails problems. Marriage entails problems. So does life with our children. Living entails problems. All human relationships do. The sooner we're honest about it, the better we'll be for our youngsters and the better we'll guide their sex education.

Certainly we can learn, but not on the basis of hiding feelings. Only on the basis of truth.

Being Honest in Our Reactions to Our Children

As we've seen, the emotional attachments which a child experiences in his home are of first importance in sex education. It is in his home that he learns most essentially about loving and being loved. It is here he gets his first experiences in the sharing of his feelings on which depends his later ability to understand another's. When he goes to school, his teachers become a kind of parent-substitute.

One question that parents and teachers ask constantly is this: "If understanding acceptance of children's feelings plays such a great role in their maturing, does this mean that we must consistently be acceptant?"

In all honesty, we know that different moments find us in different moods. Things that get us down at one time do not bother us at other times. Irritation and aggravation are bound to enter. Then, as one eight-year-old said to her mother, "Your crossnesses cross mine and we irrelate each other."

However, when the storminess passes and sympathy returns and we feel "terrible" about our touchiness, we can turn acceptant again. We can then honestly say, "I'm mad at myself for having been such an old nasty!"

Ordinarily, when a parent's honest feelings are not hidden, children feel more secure to move forward in their sexual-emotional development. They know what's what.

Carl, who is seven, says, "My father has his angry spells all right. In one way I like to see them as long as they don't get too bad. He's not as scarey as my mother. He bursts it out and gets it over and then he's nice. He's got the *out* kind of madness.

"But my mother, she's got the *in* kind. She holds onto it and keeps it from sparking. She tries to be so good all the time. But you just know that inside she's terribly angry. . . . It's more scarey that way when you can't see it. *Like being scared in the dark.* You want to run into bed and pull the covers up over your head." (Like going back to babyhood and not advancing.)

How prevent our irritation from reaching too high a peak? This is a very touchy and very tender and very important question.

Many times we can do it by

naming our own feelings as soon as we sense them smouldering in us.

Then they're not as apt to go beyond the point where they make it too hard to control our acts.

Marjorie's mother did it by saying, "I'm cross today and can't take it. I'm feeling generally mean."

"Oh," says Marjorie, recognizing the honest declaration as a confidence shared. "But tomorrow you'll be all right."

A wonderful high school teacher, usually able to listen to the feelings of his youngsters, did it also. "I've had some things that upset me outside of school and I don't feel at all like accepting your downbeats this morning. . . ."

"We'll hold them then." "We can save our gripes till you're in the mood." "Don't worry, teacher, you're okay."

Such outspokenness can often prevent more terrifyingly vehement outbursts. It is better by far, too, than either inexplicable chips on the shoulder or a martyred air of sweetness. The child is warned of the storm. He knows when it's there. And that it's best to avoid steering into its midst. He knows when it's over. Temporarily he has met the reality of not being able to sail into the sheltered harbor. But he soon learns that he can regain it safely when the waves smooth down.

Children can ordinarily take our feelings in stride as long *as we are not too violent* and *not too constantly upset,* and as long *as we do not blame them undeservedly for what has generated somewhere else.*

Says eight-year-old Delia comfortably, "My parents get mad sometimes. Just normal. It's mostly when we kids ask for it, when either of us act like brats."

In contrast, nine-year-old Bets expounds, "My mother lets it out on me when she's mad at Daddy. Why does she have to give me the wrong piece of pie? I don't like to see a big person yell at a child for not doing anything really naughty but just because they're all rigged up to get mad."

Even when a child is tiny, he senses the feelings that exist between the two adults from whom he learns most about sex and love. His parents' attachment to each other teaches him his first lessons about man–woman relationships.

A new baby is closest, of course, with his mother. But his mother reacts to his father. Their attachment to each other creates a bond that stretches like an invisible swaddling blanket to envelop the baby newly born.

Infants probably get their cues as to how we feel from the tensions we betray in our movements and in our muscles as we touch and handle them. Later, other cues enter. The slight drawing together of eyebrows. The straightening of lips. The hunching of shoulders. The ups and downs in voice. The rush and halting of speech. All these and other endless details a child picks up through his various senses. One three-year-old, for instance, declared he could always tell when his father got mad. "Not only when he yells, but when he's quiet I can tell, too." ... "How?" ... "Oh," he answered, "I can tell. He smells different. When he's mad he really smells."

We cannot fool our children.

A bright seven-year-old is quick to notice her father's slip of the tongue. "He wanted to say to my mother 'Brace up!' But instead what he said was 'Break up!' And if you ask me, that's what he meant." A two-year-old reacts with stomach upsets whenever her parents feel at daggers' points with each other even though they keep things externally smooth.

When parents try not to show how they feel toward one another, they can rest assured that the cover never really covers. Feelings seep through. Willy-nilly these are part of the child's sex education.

Then, if they hide the fact from him that there is conflict between them, he feels "out." This defeats his wish for belonging, his natural wish to feel "in."

Although a solid marriage is still the best gift we can give our children to help them grow sexually, all is not lost if the marriage should fail.

A child can tolerate parental conflict, even divorce and separation, if he is helped, for one thing, to feel that he still belongs—not to just one parent but, if possible, to both.

"We don't love each other any more and we've decided to live in different houses. Your home will be here, Gladys," a mother explained to her six-year-old. "But your Daddy will still be your Daddy. . . ."

"You won't care if I love him?"

"I'll expect you to love him although at times I probably will care."

"You mean it'll make you cross at me?"

"It'll probably make me cross. But not really at you. However, when you feel my crossness you'll get cross at me. And then I'll expect you to tell me straight out. And I hope I'll be sensible enough to say, 'I'm cross at him really and at myself for not having been able to get along better!' . . .

"And then you and I, we'll get back more quickly on regular terms!"

Where the marital conflict is basically less separating—

> *Seeing parents get back together again*
> *after brief differings*
> *is healthy sex education.*

Twelve-year-old Henriette says, for instance, "Knowing that my parents get mad at each other makes me feel normal. I'm not the only one that explodes nor the only one they explode at. And," she adds with a contented gleam in her eye, "it's kind of good to know they fight and make up!" As if there were not quite such a wide and impossible leap to accomplish between being a growing-up person and a grown-up.

A surface act, as if all were well, can make a child feel that attachments between a man and woman are somehow shallow or false.

On the other hand—

> Conflict outspokenly met and handled lets the child pick up the great and good truth that loving can be sturdy enough to withstand the flurries that inevitably come into any human relationship.

He can gather: This is how it is between a man and a woman. They can be loving and warm. They can also differ and make up solidly.

And such things carry over into the man–woman relationships he himself forms.

And so, as part of his sex education, we will need to develop franker ways and means of letting him in on such matters so that their bigness does not overwhelm him.

Telling him, in his terms, about our feelings.

Letting him ask his own questions.

Answering with honest simplicity.

Sharing what he can understand.

These are good things to do.

Obviously, children should not, however, be burdened with all the minute adult details. When these are too complex, the naming of your feelings for what they are—a simple statement that you're "upset" or "at outs"—can sufficiently illumine the path.

"Mother thinks one way; I think another and we have to talk it through alone," said a father. "You mean yell it through," his nine-year-old parried, adding shortly, "Well, if that makes you feel better, all right."

Being frankly let in on the fact that his parents have differences relieves the child of feeling that *he* may be to blame.

56

But hearing about something and witnessing something that might be assumed to be more violent than it is are two different matters. To have children actually behold violent fights, to have them hear constant bitter arguments, to listen in on a lot of details that are too intimate—all this may well be beyond a child's capacity to digest.

"Come on, Trinie. We gotta let them fight it out in peace."

The line of demarcation between what is too frightening and what a child can bear is not a sharp one. It depends for one thing on the underneath feelings within the "contestants."

One delightful family where both father and mother come from warmly open but hot-tempered backgrounds is full of warmly waged open fights. "Mama yells, Papa yells. And all of us kids, we make bets together who'll win. We know that it's not for serious. It's just their way."

In contrast another family has such bitterness between each wrangling word that the impact is frighteningly felt.

Every family needs twosomes for intimacy. Twosomes between child and parent; twosomes between the two parents in which they can have time to work things out together. Parents need privacy. Being honest does not mean letting our children be constant bystanders witnessing all. But it does mean our not obscuring that we do have our differences on occasion and that *these differences do not make everything all wrong.*

This brings a touch of down-to-earth and wholesome reality into sex education. It belies the unachievable expectations of story and myth. "They lived happily ever after" becomes a thing of flesh and coursing blood, alive and vivid. "Happiness" and "perfection" are divorced, as they well need to be if happiness is not to fail. The child can see that good, steady attachments are ones that are worked on as the inevitable hard moments arise.

Being Honest in Our Talk of Sex and in the Terms We Choose and Use

Says one mother, "I think you're supposed to use scientific terms when you talk about sex. And I try to pretend I'm comfortable that way. But in all honesty, I'm not."

It is hard to communicate with a sense of at-homeness in a foreign tongue with which one lacks familiarity. Just so in sex education: It's best to use whatever words and terms are natural and familiar.

A seven-year-old asks, "Dorothy, please tell me, why don't they use plain, simple words that a child can understand? Easier words. Like 'rump.' Why don't they say 'tummy' or 'belly' instead of 'abomination' [meaning abdomen]. And 'belly button' instead of 'navy.' And then they're so inconsiderate [inconsistent]. They pronunciate like my little sister does. They say 'womb' instead of 'room' for the baby-room inside the mother where the baby grows."

As we have said before—

SCIENTIFIC TERMS
do not guarantee
SCIENTIFIC KNOWLEDGE.

From the child's point of view, the more familiar he feels with the language, the less difficult will it be for him to put his wonderings and questions and feelings into words.

Just so with us! In fact, the more comfortable we feel, the better for him. It's no use introducing an additional note of discomfort into a subject where there are already enough hazards to being at ease and secure.

Some parents feel more comfortable in using scientific terms. Then they should use them. *Some parents feel easier with the terms they used in their own childhood or with other nursery terms.* With some parents, *the most comfortable choice of language varies with the child's age.* They prefer to use the nursery terms when their children are younger and the more scientific ones later on. Introducing synonyms gradually, using both the old term and a new one for a while, may help make the transition more relaxed for all concerned. In any event, parents will want their child to learn the scientific terms gradually as he matures. (And so we will introduce them in context as we go along.)

But most important—

If we *feel embarrassed, say that we are.*

If we don't, the child will sense it anyway. (Again honesty is best.) He will feel more comfortable, too, if we can add that our embarrassment comes from something in *us* due to the way we were brought up. Otherwise he is apt to think that there is something in *him* causing our discomfort, and that he should not bring us any more questions.

Debby, eight, says, "My father gets so embarrassed about

sex. He tries to talk sensibly but you can see he's all squinching inside and trying so hard to hide it that you get embarrassed for fear he'll find out you can see it.

"My mother's better. She gets embarrassed, too. But she didn't have much chance to talk about such things as a child. She told me that. She says she still has some trouble but we should go right ahead anyway. She'll never learn to talk better if she doesn't get any practice."

This brings us back to our own beginnings. If our attitude toward sex is not as we like it, if our response to sex is not as we want it, we need to know firmly: It is not because some innate, inborn something is wrong. We have come into this way of thinking and feeling through experiences we have had. We have come to them through what we learned as we grew. Since we were able to learn one way, we can learn another. It isn't too late.

The most important learning of all is learning to be as honest as we can with ourselves.

Being Honest with Ourselves

Being honest with oneself is not easy. No one ever manages it completely. "It's so much more comforting," says one man, "to hide what's disagreeable."

In some instances going to a professional person—psychiatrist, psychologist, family counselor, doctor, or clergyman trained in such matters—is the very best step we can take. Many parents today recognize that going for such help does not mean one is "crazy" but that one has good sense. Enrolling in classes for parents or in a psychotherapy group can also be a good move. Sometimes thinking back brings us new light, especially if we do this after we are equipped with the new realization that feelings need not always be pleasant.

Sometimes learning about ourselves comes also as we observe and listen to what our children say and feel and show.

Being Honest about Mistakes

A child once said:

"Mistakes mean
When you forget.
It's not much fun
To make them;
I'd rather not."

But who at times doesn't forget? Who at times doesn't forget the "right" way, the kind way, the firm resolution to do better? Who, looking back, can ever see a slate clean of mistakes?

"If only I hadn't!" voices a natural regret. But we do not need to feel that once a mistake is made all is lost.

In sexual development, as we've said, each period of life possesses leftovers from every period that has passed. Remnants may cling especially out of the child's early years. Old hungers may stick.

We can help to clean up leftovers and feed old hungers in appropriate fashion far better if we honestly face the mistakes we know we have made. We can let a young child, for instance, have some sucking experiences he missed out on in infancy if—like Jane's mother—we see the mistake that was made in weaning him too soon. We can feed him extra doses of loving. We can feed him joyous moments of doing things that he likes.

Actually—

The single mistake rarely matters.

The *over-all relationship counts far more.* We can, in fact, make a lot of mistakes. But if the internal feelings of *being with a child* are combined with the *willingness to let him grow* and *let him go*—nevertheless *furnishing him with*

61

our firm strength and control and support—then the single, double, triple mistake will be lost.

Its influence will diminish even more if we can admit to changes within ourselves, rather than having to "stick by our guns" in defending old attitudes.

A youngster in her teens says, " A month ago my mother and father thought it was horrible for a child to feel sexy. If I so much as mentioned a boy, they'd mutter, 'You're too young,' as if I were a lost soul. But now they see that they were mistaken. They admit it and they've learned to be different. They really feel different, you see. They say, 'It's hard to wait!' But they don't ever say any more, 'It's bad to want!' And their new understanding makes up a lot for the way they were."

Most of us feel painfully that we have "made too many mistakes." We are inclined to blame ourselves for everything. We forget that there are bound to be many tough and frightening and disappointing happenings in every child's life. We lose sight of the fact that most children manage to weather a good many such experiences without too devastating effects.

In our lifetime we are not going to be able to "do everything." But we hope we will be able to help our children acquire freer, less tradition-bound attitudes toward sex than those by which most of us were brought up. Then, in their turn, our children will be able to do more for their children, and their children for their children, so that the seed we have planted flowers more graciously with each generation's new growth.

PART 3 | SEX EDUCATION THAT GROWS WITH YOUR CHILD

6 | Sex Education in Infancy

A baby is born. His sex education begins.

What are the sort of attachments or relationships at this period of life which are essentially part of his sex education? What sort of body sensitivities enter in shaping his love life? And what can we gather about his feelings and infantile imaginings through the signs and signals he gives before words?

The Power to Receive

Love is a compound of many things. The ability to receive and accept love is important as well as the ability to give it.

One husband complained, "There's something between my wife and me that bothers me plenty. Take birthdays, for instance. She goes to no end of trouble finding out what I want and getting it for me. But if I do the same for her, there's always a comment. 'You shouldn't have done it!' Or take the evenings when I come home. She has my slippers out and the newspaper waiting with the pages all back in proper order. But if I want to help in the kitchen, it's 'No, dear! You're tired.' Or, 'Don't bother, darling.' And off she bustles. She's always got to be the giver. She's pretty uncomfortable on the receiving end."

A wife complains, "My husband can never accept compliments. He literally shudders and huddles back into himself."

Underneath such things, far back out of memory's reach,

may lie a distant distrust of love which runs on into adult sex life.

The opposite business of wanting too much can also stretch back. The restless reaching for more and more, the never satisfied searching, the greedy grabbing may express a hidden, uneasy feeling that whatever is given will not be enough. Expensive treasures may then be sought in place of simple pleasures. The value of things replaces the value of people. The capacity for enjoying with a deep sense of peace what another person gives has become disturbed. Many events in many stages of human development contribute to the power to receive love from another person—so necessary in sex. But its birth comes primarily with what follows birth.

The Feel of Things

A boy of six imagines: "When I was a baby inside my mother, it felt good all over. When she breathed she rocked me a little; when she walked she rocked me a lot. When she moved I could feel it all around me. The rocking touched all of me every bit. And when she was quiet, the quiet touched all over me too. There was no part of me left without touching. There was no part just bare."

Another child says, "When a baby gets born it feels so naked. I wonder: Did they wrap me up quickly? 'Cause my skin must have missed being wrapped in Mommy."

Francey, twelve, lies luxuriantly in a warm bathtub. "Oh, it feels wonderful! The only problem is that my face and ears have to stay cold." Suddenly she is struck with an idea that she says is "science-fictionish." She would like to be able to stay as long as she wishes under water "like a seal." Or? "Like before I was born."

Whether or not it felt "good all over" to be inside of mother is something we can only guess, dream, conjecture. Many peo-

66

ple have. What we do know, however, is that when he is born, the baby is quite helpless. He is completely dependent. He can no longer be surrounded or covered except as a mothering person now does it with her care, her holding and touch.

That babies enjoy cuddling is common observation. One mother remarks, "When I hold him and stroke him, he purrs!" And she adds, "That's how I feel when my back is rubbed." Like most of us, she still likes to be "cuddled" even when grown.

Early cuddling belongs to a person's sex education.

Through happy cuddling experiences he learns to receive love.

Mothers used to be told: "Touch your baby as little as possible. Bathe and dress him with dispatch. Don't play. Don't delay. Don't spoil him by cuddling."

Now we know better. "Touch your baby and be happy about the soft feel of him. Bathe and dress him with leisurely delight. Play and delay. And don't spoil him by not cuddling. He needs cuddling a lot." This is an early gift his mother gives him to contribute to his later sexual adjustment.

Mouths Seek Answers Long Before Speech

Probably on a deep level, when a baby is held and nurtured, he feels less torn from his former shelter. The internal oneness with mother is replaced by the external oneness which she proffers with her protecting body's embrace and which he receives with his small body's dependence. It has been pointed out often in recent years that this giving and receiving can come very simply and completely as a baby is nursed.

A baby cries. Mother appears. Lifts him. Holds him to her. Feeds him from the warmth of her breast. In this act she can give him sustenance and pleasure, nourishing him physically and emotionally all at once. Or, if she cannot nurse, she approximates this in the giving of the bottle, holding the baby so

67

that he gets as much body closeness as he can. Her over-all feeling, her own satisfaction in her baby and in his satisfactions, is the most important.

He sucks. He takes in. Whereas he has been hungry and consequently distressed, his hunger now ceases. He feels comforted, comfortable, relaxed, and sleepy. The answer he has sought to well-being has come through his mouth. He has asked with his mouth and with the only sounds of which he is capable, namely his cry. With his mouth he has received another's gifts.

Doris, an imaginative and poetic child of eight, sees a neighbor's baby nurse. Through her own vivid capacity for identification, she carries herself back in a way to her own infancy and then returns wholesomely to the present. "When I was a baby," she says, "it must have felt *smooth* to eat like that. Both ways smooth. Like you say smooth to mean 'keen' and smooth to mean gentle and like velvet. Like warm water when you slide your hand through it. And like a purple pansy petal feels on your lips.

"You don't have to crunch or chew. It slides in. You don't have to reach. You don't have to even pick up your fork. It's all given to you. You can be so easily lazy. You don't have to do a single thing. Sometimes I'd like to be like that. But then, at my age I'd get terribly bored."

Nonetheless, at her age and at any age, unless we have built too rigid bulwarks against them, most of us do enjoy, as one man put it, "the delicious leftovers" that remain to us of infantile satisfactions.

The lazy indolence of stretching, half sunk in soft sand. The smooth feel of ice cream on a hot day, sliding down. The ability to enjoy "liquid sunshine," the "wind's caresses," and to accept and take in the powerful sweetness of a beloved person's touch. . . .

Not only does the baby need to suck for food intake. He needs to suck too for the intake of feeling cared for and loved.

And for the hearty and good perception of bodily well-being that he gets.

Thus—

Early feeding experiences belong to sex education.
Through happy ones a child learns to take in love.

Just as a child in arms finds his world of oneness with mother in one important way through his mouth, so for many months he seeks to find oneness through his mouth with many other things in his world. Including himself.

Into his mouth go blanket and rattle, toy dog and bottle. Especially fingers and toes. He *takes in* things, as it were like food, with his mouth. Makes them a part of himself. Strange no longer.

Beep, who is eight months old, pulls himself into upright position by clutching the seat of a chair. He stands shakily, whimpering slightly, tottering mightily. Then his head goes forward and his lips find the edge of the chair seat. His mouth opens and he sucks on the foam rubber upholstery. And with this mouth contact, he stands steady. Suddenly secure.

Obviously the grasp of his mouth could not be as steadying physically as the grip of his hands. But it is more emotionally steadying. As result, his body action responds to his good body-feelings. His whole deportment steadies.

He lifts his head, pats the chair, and smiles broadly out at the world. It's as if he were saying, "I took you in. I got hold of you through my mouth. That helped me feel steady. You're a nice chair now." In a way it seems as if he has identified the chair with the mother in a primitive wish-fantasy to "take in" so as not to feel strange and lonely in a big world of as-yet-unfamiliar people and things.

By doing this with many objects, he gains the needed feeling of taking in and of knowing. He gets the feel of familiarity. He may even try to know people by putting their thumbs into his mouth. But he discovers gradually that another is neither food nor mother. In the same way even mother grows to be other-than-himself.

She comes. She goes. The more *one* he has felt with her earlier, the more readily can he begin to separate her from himself. The more readily can he feel himself as a small still-dependent person, *himself* nevertheless, and his mother as that other so much needed being, so familiar to him, who loves, who gives, and whom he can trust.

In adult sex life we still have holdovers of this.

You fall in love. You drink in the other person, as it were. You take in every facet. You identify. It is as if the two of you were one. Then as you go on together, you begin to note differences. Your beloved is not you; but other-than-you. However, you still have interchange that feeds and enriches your soul. You take in the values offered and give of yourself in return.

The taking-in process has led out far and wide. To take in. To know. To become familiar with. To become at home with. To feel at one with. To discover another as other-than-yourself. All of these are basic to sound loving. They start when one is an infant. In short, friendship and loving begin with taking in —or receiving and accepting—another person.

When Not Enough Infant Joy

We have heard of rooming-in, of having the newborn infant in the room with his mother so that she may reach out for him whenever he voices his wishes. But many hospitals do not provide for this. And some mothers feel the need of being assured of more rest for themselves. Even so, they may go to no end of trouble to arrange for rooming-in. But this is sheer folly. For rooming-in does no one any good when a mother chooses it as a kind of duty, underneath wishing the baby elsewhere.

When a woman has a baby, a part of her yearns to be a baby herself, both during pregnancy and during the days after the

70

baby is born (as Mary's doctor explained). Being mothered herself, by her husband especially, is often what she needs most to give her baby the mothering he needs.

Breast-feeding is another thing that we know can contribute to a baby's security. And yet, many a mother finds it difficult. "I ought to like it," says one, "I ought to but I can't."

Daughter: "When I grow up I'm going to have a hundred babies."
Father: "Why, dear?"
Daughter: "Because when you're having a baby, that's the easy time to be cross in. No one gets cross back at you. They just give you things."

Usually the feeling of not liking to nurse reaches back into childhood. Talking about the whole matter with one's doctor before the baby's birth can sometimes ease the inner doubts enough to make nursing "feel good," as indeed it should. In fact, it is frequently the fear of letting it feel good that stands in a mother's way.

In its turn this fear may relate to earlier fears and fantasies in her life connected with old body pleasures. In any event, when fear or doubt or a sense of not liking to nurse remain in the mother, the baby is apt to get the tension that runs from her mind through her muscles. Then he may feel *as if she were shoving instead of loving him.* And the sense of oneness in nursing is lost. Even though she cannot help realizing that if things were different neither mother nor baby would have to miss out on an experience that would be fulfilling for both, nevertheless from the point of view of sexual-emotional development, it is far better to bottle-feed the baby with a sense of enjoyment than to breast-feed him in pain. For it is the mother's feelings of joy in being one with the baby that lets him feel most comfortably one with her.

There is still another, more difficult thing that may enter to disturb the oneness of baby and mother. In our culture and in our day of turmoil and struggle, there are many women who do not want babies or who are unready to have them when they find themselves pregnant. This is something one cannot own up to to one's child. It would be too devastating. But owning up to it to oneself and, if possible, getting professional help is better than denial.

Janet, as example, joined a group of mothers whose discussions were led by a psychologist. Knowing how important it was to be honest, she was very forthright about how she felt. "I'm furious at myself, for I didn't want a baby. I just didn't. And yet, in spite of contraceptives, I had her. I hated it, I'll tell you. But I've got her. And that's that. I can't sell myself a bill of goods and say I adore it now that she's here. So I weep to John every so often about how irked I am. And then I do better. And I've been better still since I've been talking about it here. I see how cute she really is."

Another matter that calls for honest admission has to do with one's feeling concerning the sex of a child.

Are his father and mother glad that he's a boy? Are they pleased to have a little girl? Or do they feel that the child they got is only second best, not really what they wanted? From this he can begin to sense that being a male or female is either a liability or an asset. And out of this can come an individual's feeling about his own desirability as a man or woman. And envy, too, toward a partner who is what he could not be but wanted to be, perhaps all unconsciously, in order to have his attachment with mother or father or both count for more.

"If I'd been the boy my folks wanted, they would have loved me," says one wife. "Maybe that's why I'm having such a time with my marriage. My husband says I always have to wear the pants."

To cope with such problems, seeking professional help is usually again the best course.

But to return to simpler matters, there is another thing which we have learned may contribute to trusting that one will receive nourishing love. It is to feed a baby by what has been called a "self-demand" schedule, when he is hungry rather than by the clock. For some mothers, however, this too is hard. Perhaps the mother's sense of having had too many demands in her own childhood makes it difficult now to take into account another's demands as generously as she otherwise might. If she tries to play the martyr or follows the baby's demands out of a sense of duty, the result, so far as sex education is concerned, is to make the act of receiving uncomfortable and tense. It's better by far to have her doctor help her work out some compromise that lets her feel comfortable. For the baby's comfort and his oneness with her depends more on her true comfort than on any heroic effort she may make.

If we are realistic, we can admit that, like any normal person, a newborn's mother is bound to have normal moments of irritation or "nerves." Feelings of being overburdened at times naturally arise. To have two people's wishes completely fit into one another's at all moments, even if they are mother and baby, is practically impossible.

To satisfy the baby completely at all times *is* impossible, as was brought out earlier. For a baby wishes to have *all:* all of mother, all of comfort, all of life without cold or hunger or pain. However, the *more* he can have in infancy, the easier it becomes to endure *less* later.

"I see," says one mother. "It's natural for a baby to want everything. So, when an adult is a selfish person, he's a normal infant but he's not a normal adult. In moments when I want something and my baby wants something else, it helps me to remember that!"

Some mothers obviously are "easier-going" than others. They can take the infant's wants more in stride. Others find them more difficult. Their own dispositions, their own backgrounds, the satisfactions they get in their marriages, all enter. The sensitivity to pain and to frustration with which their infant is endowed enters too. What proves gravely upsetting to one infant may leave another undisturbed.

The need to suck, for instance, seems to be stronger in certain infants than in others. When they are not allowed to suck it out, as it were, their protest and anger are stronger.

Weaning, too, brings differing reactions. For every baby, however, it means essentially giving up mother as well as foregoing very enjoyable infant body pleasure. It carries with it, therefore, some sense of being deprived. But for one baby this may be far easier than for another.

All other things being equal, if his mother has enjoyed him, talked with him, played with him, smiled and gooed and cooed with him—he will, when the time comes, be readier to reach out for a face, for a toy, for a toe, or for father's arms as separate joys to replace mother-as-part-of-him.

Even so, with any baby it is best to go about the weaning

process gradually. It is helpful to observe his reactions carefully when he is called on to give up breast or bottle and to give due regard to his protests, not pushing or pressing him to move too fast. Dropping it for a while. Coming back to it later, even a week later, may avoid an issue that carries too much frustration and pain. It's a good idea, too, to give him extra doses of cuddling at other than feeding times to offset what he is giving up.

Only the baby knows if he has enough food or cuddling, sucking or loving. Only the baby can feel if for him his oneness with mother has lasted long enough.

On the other hand, a mother can cling and inadvertently hold the baby too long. To many a mother the comfort of a baby's warm closeness means such a lot in her insecure days that she yearns to hold onto holding him. Through her attachment with him she may, moreover, be striving to get closeness that she herself has needed since her own infancy.

Mary found that she was doing this very thing with her baby, Tommy. "I guess my mother was unhappy with my father and abstracted with me. I think, really, when my father was still physically in the house with us, he was absent emotionally so much of the time that when he left us it added only his physical absence. Mother tried to handle the situation. She tried so hard. She was a good mother. But she was withdrawn and absent too.

"And then, big Tom, being as unable as he was at first to give me closeness, I got to hanging onto little Tom to give me everything I'd missed. It was the biggest wrench to give up nursing. My nuzzling little nursing-Tommy was like a part of me I hated to lose.

"In fact I loved every bit of his babyness. I didn't like it, if I'm honest, when he started to walk off with that air of independence. I didn't like it when he began following in Tom's trail, leaving me out. . . .

75

"And that made awful trouble for Tommy. He'd been so contented and darling when he and I both were happily clinging. But when he needed to try out his unsteady steps to grow steadier and I tried to keep him wrapped up in me, he ran. Talk about restless! He even got out of bed and ran around at night as if something were after him. He was afraid, I guess, that I'd grab him back and hang onto him like a leach.

"I didn't see it, though, till I went for professional help. And then I certainly did. I saw Tommy years from now dashing from one woman to another, afraid to stay too long with any one for fear they'd hang onto him like his mother."

We've heard so much, though, about the desirability of giving a baby closeness that we may keep on with too much of it for too long and not let him go to grow at his own pace. Being there with open arms when he needs us is important still for many years. But not feeling that we are failing because he is walking and talking and wanting to try things out in his own funny ways, jumping down from our laps, no longer needing the oneness with mother that he needed before.

Some mothers inadvertently cling to their children by continuing to put too much emphasis on food and feeding. "You have to eat this!" "You mustn't eat that!" "This is good for you. It doesn't matter if you don't like it, you have to eat it anyway!"

"Oh dear," mutters eleven-year-old Marjorie, "it's as if even your taster weren't your own!"

For sound sex education—

We need inwardly to *let go* of clinging to a child as a baby.

We need to *let him grow* at his own pace.

It's never too late to start letting go when we discover that we have been clinging in some way.

Viewed from the Infant Mind

As we've seen, there are times in every baby's life when satisfactions are delayed or interfered with. His whimpering

76

cry then grows louder. More demanding. Angrier. He does not nuzzle gently. He does not touch mother's breast with hands restfully rounded. His body does not relax in curved repose. He stiffens. He pushes. He pulls. He grunts. He clamps his jaws, clutches with fists, digs in with his nails. It's as if he were trying to get the whole of mother into himself.

Mother: "Now Henry, eat your cereal. Tuck in your napkin. Take more applesauce. Put on some cream. . . ."
Big sister to herself: "If she could safety-pin him to her, she would. Doesn't she realize he's getting old?"

In adulthood, some people still appear to have leftovers of these babyhood phases. Along with the wish-fantasy to be one again by being inside mother, they may unconsciously fantasy becoming one with mother by a kind of belated devouring. Sawyer, now married, as a child had never had enough, he reported. "This morning in bed I gave my wife a love bite. I said, 'I'd like to eat you up, I love you so much.'" He pondered a moment and added with a sudden burst into consciousness of thoughts he had not known were there, "Then I'd have sole possession of her. No one else would have an in. I want to absorb her completely. Have her all to myself. Sometimes I think, too: If I can't get her, let her get me. Make me be inside her. Back in the baby state inside her." Then angrily, "She'd *have* to feed me; she'd have to take me everywhere with her. Either way, I'd be the only one."

Such expressions come like the spurting of a volcano out of the abyss of infancy. Children, who are closer in time span, show in vivid dreams and fantasies the same sort of thing.

A boy of eight paints a picture of a tiny boy in bed with a gigantic figure of a "dream monster" rising out of his head. He says, "I dreamed it had sharp teeth and sharp edges everywhere," as indeed it has in his picture. "He's my friend. He carries out my designs. He goes and eats the mother. The monster gobbles her for me!"

But another side of the picture often crops up—the fear of having her eaten and gone.

Little Elsa, who has been quite disturbed by the arrival of a small brother, happens to be in a nursery school where her teacher understands childhood fantasies. One day Elsa takes a hunk of clay. She calls it "Mama." She points to some projections and asks, "Is this her breasts?" and without waiting to be answered starts scratching at the humps. "You bad Mama. I don't like you. The baby bites her. She made a deep hole in her [making herself into the baby and using her nails as teeth]. I'll chop you to chop suey and I'll eat you down inside me. Now I got you." Then she sits back on her haunches and looks puzzled. "Where is my Mama?" she asks. "She's gotta come back and cook my dinner. You naughty girl, don't you eat Mama up."

"The little girl is angry and wants to eat her Mama. But she can't," says her teacher, separating feeling from act, and fantasy from reality. And Elsa with a look of relief echoes, "No, she can't."

Many times there enters, too, the fear of the mother's doing to the child what the child would like to do to the mother. Thus *the child pins his own wish-fantasy onto the other person.* (This is what Sawyer had done.)

Bill, five, does it also. He plays, for example, with some rubber animals. The baby bear goes up to the mother bear and nudges her. "Nibble, nibble," says Bill softly. Then louder. "The mean old thing walks away." "Grnnff! He's on her. Crunch! he bites! Pounce! he claws!"

There follows much snapping of teeth to imitate bear bites, many clawings. But suddenly everything stops. Bill's hands go slack. "The mama bear!" he mutters. "She says, 'You're a bad one!' She said, 'I'll eat you.' And she did." And very low, "Then there wouldn't be any more me."

In short, Bill has identified the baby bear with himself. In his imagination, to punish him, the mother bear gobbled him up in the same manner that he had imagined doing to her.

Curious though it may seem—

A child's fantasies of eating and being eaten can color his concepts concerning intercourse and impregnation, pregnancy and birth.

From such fantasies we begin to understand Steven's thinking that the baby inside the mother is "next to the toast." Babies want to eat mothers. Mothers want to eat babies. So, when a child hears that the baby grows inside mother, what is more natural than for him to conclude that the baby got there by some swallowing process?

Peggy, three, has been told with careful explanation that babies grow in a "special place inside the mother." And yet when she sees a picture of a mother dog with a litter of puppies inside the uterus, she shows that the explanation has made very little impression. Her own version has stuck. "The mother ate the babies!" she says.

And Jack, seven, who had been asking about the father's part and had been told that the daddy has some little tiny

79

cells called sperm cells stored in his body and that one of these starts an egg cell in the mother growing into a baby, came to the conclusion quickly, "I see. The mother eats the father cell and then one of hers grows."

Similarly Nina decides that the baby growing inside her mother had been placed there by her daddy in a way spun by her own observations embroidered by her mind's imagining. She explains this seriously to her dog. "You see, Taffy, my Mommy ate my Daddy's fish and the fish went into her tummy and grew into a baby and soon the baby'll come out."

Stella as a child imagined on hearing about sexual intercourse that when a man put his penis in a woman, to use her own phrase, "It stayed in her." She wondered mightily, "How does he get it back on himself?"

To her, intercourse was an eating-up act. Then Stella grew and married. "Only," she said, "I get cold when we make love. I'm afraid in my stomach. I'm afraid that somehow, some way I'm going to hurt Bob. And, well, I told you, I just get cold." (Here Stella, like Lisa, whom we heard about earlier, has extended her mouth-wishes not only from teeth to nails clamping but to fantasies of clamping off part of another's body with the vaginal walls.)

When parents know that sex education starts in infancy, they can begin at the beginning with their children. They can carry them through step by step. But very seldom do we think of sex education this early. And so, when we do begin to focus on it, there may be baby leftovers that need belated attention. What then? we wonder. What can we do about the baby remnants that call for help after babyhood is past?

7 | Sex Education for the Leftovers from Babyhood

There are baby parts in all of us. Although forgotten, their influence runs on. Without them, we would not get some of the good pleasures and enrichments of life.

Take the pleasure of eating delectable dishes. This, in a fashion, recaptures the original baby delight in an appropriate adult way. The vast number of cookbooks published over the years attests to our interest. So do the rows of fine restaurants in any sizable city.

Nor is food the only thing we take in, as we've seen. Our appetite grows as we grow. It spreads and enlarges. We take in knowledge as a baby takes in food, and perhaps with equal eagerness. We take in the fragrance of roses or lilacs through nose instead of mouth. We take in the sound of chimes on the church tower or windbells on a swaying branch or the music of a beloved's voice as we took in the sound of Mother coming to us with satisfying response. We take in the feelings of a person we love through identification with that person— through taking in how he feels—and this enables us to give love all the better.

In contrast, we may be bothered by the persistence of unwanted infantile remnants.

You say, for instance, "I want to stop smoking or nibbling; and yet I keep going after that cigarette or tender morsel." . . .

"I ought to get up earlier; then I'd avoid rushing; and yet I snuggle down under the covers to get that extra bit of being warmly enveloped." . . . "I know I shouldn't claw at my cuticle or snap at my husband, but I do."

We can see more clearly now where these things started. But because we have lost the "feeling" connections from consciousness they have come to be out of our control. Perhaps the unwanted need to nibble constantly goes back to having been hungry in childhood for some emotional foodstuff. For love perhaps to comfort us in forgotten moments of baby distress. And now in moments of worry or distress we still turn to eating more than at other times, using physical food uncomfortably (or too fatteningly) in place of the emotional nourishment we yearned for once upon a time.

Suppose, as parents, we wake up after our child's babyhood is over to the fact that he has not had enough of the positive attachments he craves in infancy. Or enough of the good body-feelings we now know he needed. What then?

Making Up for Baby Wishes Is Part of Sex Education

As Myra Brown put it, "I get so discouraged—I did all the wrong things. I didn't nurse my children. I didn't cuddle them. I kept them on a rigid schedule. I didn't let them suck. I pulled things out of their mouths constantly. But now that Benjie's eight and Sue is four, what can I do? Am I finding all of this out too late?"

As we said earlier, it's never too late to be honest and to share feelings—both present and past.

And so Myra said to her children one evening after a particularly rough day, "You know, I think you two get real, real mad at me over lots of things. Today, for example. . . ."

"Yes," Benjie jumped in, "when you said, 'No more TV.' . . ."

"I got mad too," echoed Sue.

82

"Like you used to, I think, when you were babies and I'd say, 'No more holding.' Or, 'No more rocking or cuddling!' Or like you feel now, Sue, when I've kept picking at you to take your thumb out of your mouth?"

"You mean you're sorry?" asked Sue with wide eyes.

"Yes, darling, I am. Babies, I've learned, need lots of sucking and cuddling and holding. . . ."

"Yes," from Sue, interrupting, "I know, Mommy." And then Sue proposed a solution, "But it's okay, Mommy. You can lap-sit me now."

Benjie, however, felt with his eight-year-old masculinity that he was past his lap-sitting days.

"Perhaps," said Myra, "you can draw some pictures of what you imagine you wanted when you were a baby. Or tell me a story about it."

"Or write a story in cursive writing?" which was his newest eight-year-old skill. Thus he put the baby wishes in a fashion fitting and appropriate to his age and stage.

If we feel ourselves ready to do so, we can take some simple, tangible steps to announce, as it were, to our children that we are ready to listen and hear their voices. For example, when there is a new baby up the street or in the family, we can ponder aloud, "Don't you wonder what a baby wants? What it likes its mother to do for it and with it? . . ." This opens the door for the child's wish-fantasies to come out if he cares to bring them.

**The child who can be
OPEN WITH HIS PARENTS ABOUT HIS WISHES
is more apt later to be
OPEN WITH HIS MATE.**

Schools can help also. In a nursery school, for example, Joanne shows a hungry greed that goes back to unsatisfied baby mouth-wishes. In the way of small children, she does this through her play rather than through words. She wants one fingerpaint jar, all of it. And another and another. Every single one. She grabs. She hoards. She grabs some more. She wants all the blocks. All the dolls. All the animals.

"She's greedy," says Paul from his greater height of six months' superiority.

"She's greedy; she's needy," thinks Mrs. Swaine, her observant teacher.

And so Mrs. Swaine moves her low chair up beside the spot where Joanne is gathering her loot. "Let's see how much you have, Joanne!"

"I want all how much! I want 'em all!" with downright honesty.

"I know you want more and more and more and more. . . ."

"Yes," says Joanne with positiveness.

"Joanne wants how much and how much? Joanne wants more and more. More paints. More blocks. More dollies too. More and more and more," in a kind of chant, echoing what the child feels.

Joanne looks up, small face wistful.

"And most of all," Mrs. Swaine continues, "Joanne wants more love." She opens her arms. And Joanne climbs in, the tense little body suddenly relaxed.

"Can't have more and more toys," says Mrs. Swaine. "Got to share them. Can only have one paint, two paints, three paints. One doll. Two. And this many blocks." She helps Joanne count them when Joanne climbs down. "But as *many* hugs as you want."

"One. Two. A hundred?" Joanne wonders.

"A hundred or more."

In another school, in a second-grade room, Bruce, seven, takes a package of gum out of his pocket. Absent-mindedly

84

he stuffs one piece after another into his mouth until the whole package is in.

His very perceptive teacher, Mrs. Martin, knows that children's sexual progress may be aided if they can obtain appropriate satisfactions belatedly for wants that have not been fully met. However, she says nothing immediately. She has learned the art of observing first.

An hour later Bruce still has the gum in his mouth. Watching, Mrs. Martin notes: He does not chew it. He sucks.

How many children in this room, she glances around, how many children do suck in one way and another. Fingers. Knuckles. Erasers. The tip of a pencil. The tip of a tongue.

In "sharing time" she always let her children share their feelings as well as their doings. In line with this she says today, "Suppose we talk about how good it feels to put things in your mouths and suck them. . . ." Identifying and naming and putting into words the feelings she has observed, and opening them up for the children to talk about.

Bruce is one of the first. His mouth is still full of gum. This he tucks in the side of his cheek after rolling it around to test its feel. "To suck lemon drops is hard and cold. To suck gum is good and soft. Warm. It gives to your sucking. It changes shape like your mouth needs. So it fits."

"Jujubes feel softish, too," says Marion.

"They're next best."

"Ice cream does, too, but not sherbet. Sherbet's thin-feeling; it leaves nothing to your tongue."

"And Flav-r Straws are good to suck."

"My little brother likes to suck them like my father sucks cigars."

"And my little brother sucks his thumb. . . ."

"Maybe some of you did, too, when you were little. But now you're too big to suck your thumbs and too little to suck cigars. . . ."

85

"It's hard," mutters Bruce.

"Yes," says Mrs. Martin, "it's very frustrating."

They grin. They've heard the word before. Its bigness makes them feel big.

Getting Baby Angers Out of the Way

Mrs. Martin senses her opportunity here to get to the angry feelings which, when piled too high, form barriers against loving-sexual expression. She recognizes this as an important part of what an understanding teacher can do in sex education. And so she goes on, "You know when something's very frustrating how it makes you feel?"

"Mad!"

"Cross!"

"Angry."

"Mean."

"Like grabbing things to get even."

(Spontaneously identifying the feelings of anger that grow out of unfulfilled wishes.)

"Maybe you'd like to paint some pictures about how it is to be a baby, about what you'd really like and enjoy and want to have if you were a baby. Or about how angry you'd be and what you'd want to do if you didn't get it." (Opening the door for imaginings that hold over from infancy to come out if the children want to bring them.)

"You mean like my little brother does when he yells and scratches and bites. . . ."

"Or like if you were a wild animal. . . ."

"Yes."

"Or a wild person," from Nanette, the quietest child.

"Yes, all those things."

They get to work.

One paints a peaceful picture of a mother in a rocking chair holding a baby close, obviously nursing, her breasts large. (The

86

best baby-wish, thinks Mrs. Martin.) Another does a line drawing full of action: a baby again. But this baby is rushing headlong at its mother, its teeth enormous. "Grrrrr" comes out of its mouth in a great rising growl, slanting to the top of the paper. (Baby biting-hostility here!) And Nanette, who has suggested drawing a wild person, does a crayon picture of a very large, very fat child with a tremendous red mouth, all set to eat up a man and woman half its size. This she labels, "Canibull Baby" and gazes at it with pride.

"Only you know you cannot do that. You can think it and imagine it, of course. But you cannot do it!" says Gunther, looking at it in "sharing time" when Mrs. Martin asks Nanette if she would like to hold it up to discuss with the others.

"That's right," says Mrs. Martin. "You can say your feelings out or you can paint them out or write poems about them. You can do certain things with them along certain channels" (defining the *hows*).

"Like you turn your TV to certain channels and the picture makes a good picture. But if you turn it on other channels it's all junked up and it makes a lot of trouble for your eyes and ears."

"Yes," agrees Mrs. Martin, "just like that. You get yourselves into trouble if you don't choose proper channels. And you know too, that certain channels are all right in certain places only and at certain times only. You can, for instance, talk about these feelings in sharing time but not in arithmetic time" (helping to define the *whens*).

"And not in the other school where I went last year," put in Ray (adding his bit to defining the *wheres*).

"And in the other school you couldn't chew gum."

"In a lot of schools you're not allowed to. And then it's better to abide by the rules of the place. But our principal in this school says you can have gum here if your parents permit it."

"She's a very understanding woman, my mother says."

The ideal time for imagining how a baby feels is, of course, when a new baby is expected in the family.

Visiting a baby—if there is none at home—brings opportunities also and will perhaps open the door.

"That baby was happy while we were there but sometimes babies do get cross too." Or, "He was so furious, what do you suppose he wanted to do?"

Many times, however, no such questions are needed. A willing ear, set to attentive listening—always the emphasis on listening!—catches what it has failed to hear before.

So That Infancy's Fears Need Not Be Too Persistent

Take Roger, for instance, when he returned one day from across the street where his friend had a six-month-old baby brother.

"That crazy baby!" Roger giggled in silly abandonment.

His mother paused over the dishes. She'd heard that note in Roger's voice before when he'd come home from the neighbor's. But she'd never paid much attention to it. If she had, she would no doubt have scolded impatiently. However, since the lecture she'd been to yesterday, she'd been wondering if the nightmares that had started recently might not be Roger's means of bringing out the fears. Perhaps now she could help him get out his feelings in some less disturbing way.

"That baby?" she repeated, showing her attentiveness.

"That baby!" Roger reiterated, giggling again. "That crazy baby. It bites those big old crummy buzzooms off its mother," in a kind of hysterical, fearful delight.

Behind Roger's infantlike lack of control, his mother glimpsed the pressure of his own fictions. "Yes," she remembered, "children's angry imaginings can make them panicky."

And so she did not pounce on Roger for being silly. She did not take him to task for his "nasty thoughts." Instead she said, "Babies do *want* to do that sometimes. When they get angry

88

at their mothers" (naming the feeling and naming the object). "But," very definitely, "they can't *really* bite their mother's bosoms off." (Showing that there are limits as to how feelings can be carried out.)

"Oh," said Roger, suddenly sober, "oh, I can't, can I? Not really." As if he had just discovered an unheard of but steadying thing.

When Thumb-Sucking Has Become His Own Answer

Sometimes a child finds his own way of expressing infancy's leftover feelings through sucking his thumb. Both the wishes and the angers can be channeled out through this act. Poor handling may make him cling to it more tenaciously. Or it may make him give it up but at too great an emotional price. What parents do about thumb-sucking will, of course, depend on how they feel as well as on what they know about the facts concerning it.

In another nursery school, Timmy Thomas rests on his cot sucking his thumb. Mrs. Thomas, who is visiting today, appears worried. Later she talks with the teacher. "Is it all right to let them suck their thumbs?"

"It worries you that we let them!"

"Yes, it does. He looks so dumb. Just like I used to look on my baby pictures. Actually I was the dumbest one in my home. . . ." Mrs. Thomas breaks off.

"Some people," she resumes, "recommend pacifiers so I gave Timmy one. But whenever his two little cousins come over they each make a grab for it and put it in their mouths, and then Timmy grabs it back and it's a regular merry-go-round of pacifier turn-taking. So I didn't relish the thought from a hygienic standpoint, you know, of letting Timmy bring the thing to nursery school. Not if the others here are like his cousins. Anyway he seems to prefer his thumb."

Together Mrs. Thomas and the teacher explore the matter further. The teacher agrees that thumbs are preferable to pacifiers although she indicates that opinion varies. Her point is that children need to feel comfortable in the resources their own bodies possess for obtaining satisfactions.

Some children suck their thumbs to round out their primitive need for sucking. They may be among those who were born with a particularly strong sucking urge. They may have

Father, from between his teeth, disgustedly: "What? Sucking again?"
Sonny: "But why can't I, too?"

been fed at too widely spaced intervals or weaned too soon for their own particular sucking needs to have been gratified. They may have gulped their food so fast they got short-changed on the sucking end. So now they need to "suck it out" belatedly in order to pass on to wanting more grown-up forms of body satisfaction.

In addition, they may be sucking their thumbs to take care of leftover baby yearnings for the close mother-attachments which were originally connected with those moments when cuddling and feeding brought the greatest closeness in life. Then, extra doses of mother given appropriately may make a child readier to give up his thumb. Cuddling time, if he is still in the lap-sitting stage, is one such measure. Another, appropriate at any stage, consists of ten- or fifteen-minute twosomes with mother, repeated daily, for intimate play and sharing and talk.

Fortunately we know now that thumb-sucking will do no permanent harm to mouth or jaws if it is discarded before the permanent teeth come in. Whatever thumb-caused crookedness exists appears to correct itself at this time so that straightening teeth mechanically is on the average no more frequent in children who have been thumb-suckers than in children who have not. In other words, the eventual straightness of teeth and normalcy of jaw formation seem to be matters of heredity rather than of anything else. If a child gives up his thumb in time and if his genes grant him a well-formed mouth, the earlier sucking will not have hurt.

Moreover, the best way to have thumb-sucking stop on time is to let it run its course. However, if a child's anger has piled up, he may continue to use his thumb not only as a source of comfort or pleasure but as a weapon. As one six-year-old gleefully exclaimed, "When I suck it's such fun to see my mother have fits."

Helping a child find ways of rerouting his anger often turns the tide. Giving the child many chances to bring it out more directly makes the indirect sucking-thumb method less necessary.

In no cases are restraints and painful gadgets called for. These may stop the sucking but they bring on such discomfort that the comforting value of sucking is doubly sought. They also make anger grow to where more far-reaching problems result. They may make fear mount to terrifying proportions. A child, for instance, into whose mouth a dentist had fastened a kind of dental plate with sharp prongs called a "hayrake," found the pointed edges jagging his thumb when he climbed into bed and sought his accustomed comfort. He went into a paroxysm of panic and rage intermingled. "The crocodile," he kept screaming.

To the psychologist he finally confided after months of irrationally fearful behavior, "They put those teeth in my mouth because she didn't like it. And the crocodile, the mother, the crocodile—she was going to bite off my thumb." To him, the mother and the crocodile were one. And his fear-fantasies told him that his mother was hurting him as punishment for being "bad."

It is not often so dramatic. But it is nonetheless always *hurtful from the point of view of a child's sex education if he comes to feel "bad" for getting body pleasure of this sort*. For it lays the foundation to feeling later that any sort of body pleasure is "bad."

What we have been pointing out is, in brief, that when left-over mouth-wishes or angers run on untended, various problems beside thumb-sucking may ensue. A youngster may turn nail-biter, for one thing. Or later he may grow into the kind of person who must spoil intimate relationships with biting remarks. Note how we talk in such terms as "biting wit," "devouring sarcasm," "snapping" at one's spouse, "scratching out" an old sweetheart (using nails in the same way as teeth).

Fortunately, as we've seen, opportunities to work out at least some of the push of such feelings are possible in childhood as a part of sex education. Then they won't have to be projected later into inappropriate and needless bouts of ripping apart an undeserving husband or wife.

Clearing the Way for Sex Information to Take

By now it has become clear to us that although every life is essentially different, there are certain very basic, elemental strands that run through most.

To sum this up very briefly in relation to infancy:

Every baby feels every few hours, "I am hungry." This is universal. From it comes the wish: "I want to take in through my mouth."

Every baby also feels: "I am helpless." This too is universal. And so there follows naturally in every baby: "I wish to be cuddled and held."

Out of his universal need for food and his universal need to rely on a mothering person comes the wish to be one with her.

Out of wishes and hungers that can never fully be met grows that universal and most natural anger which the baby wants to discharge as best he can and with what equipment he has; with jaws that clamp, and a little later with tooth and nail.

No wonder, then, that the same basic threads are found so often running through the fantasies that children carry over from infancy.

What we said earlier (in Chapter 4) can be more clearly seen now: The fantasies which the child makes up are like his own stories. He weaves them out of wishes, angers, and fears related to his attachments and body-feelings. His fantasies are his fairy tales which he concocts for himself. But all too frequently he takes them mistakenly for truths by which to live. All too frequently he weaves them into his concepts concerning sex and sexual processes. And then his fictions distort the scientific information and the facts that we bring.

There are two parts to taking care of old fantasies:

To get old feelings out through various safe channels. This is of first importance. It is the part we have been discussing.

Our next step is:

To include in sex information—
not facts alone
but a *comparison of
fantasies and facts.*

It is like this: You have some old dresses you've shoved into a drawer and haven't looked at for years. And yet you are nostalgic for them. They have an aura about them that makes you cling to them. You have a feeling that you can pull them out at any time and put them on and wear them fittingly.

And then you do take them from their hiding place and you lay them side by side, the old next to the new. And the contrast stands out quite clearly. You breathe a sigh of relief, "Oh well! I don't have to hang onto those old things any longer! They're outmoded. I can pitch them. I can let them go."

Just so with sex: The old idea in which a child has clothed himself can either be left in the drawer to get outmoded. Or it can be taken out to be compared with the facts. When he says, for instance, "Where did I come from?" or "Where do babies grow?" and you say, "From a special place inside the mother" —you leave his ideas in the drawer.

Sometime later you go on, "A special place inside the mother's body called the uterus. . . ." It's a term he's never heard. Again you have done nothing to *compare his own fictions with correct facts*. He is thrown back into what he has in his own mind: "Inside the mother? In the mother's inside? A special place? Oh, yes!" and his old eating fantasies fill the gap. "Oh, yes!" *Even if you haven't mentioned "stomach" his mind has.*

In addition, to most children "stomach" also means the whole front wall of the body. As Tony said, "You've got a skin-stomach where you put your finger in your belly button. And back of that you've got an eating-stomach where you put your milk." *Unless you make it clear which of his stomachs you mean, the "special place where the baby grows" or the "uterus" is apt to mean to him the eating place.* The remnants of his baby imaginings about being one with mother, about eating and being eaten have made the decision for him and have gotten the matter all confused. (Out of this, as we've seen, later sexual problems may develop.) It's better not to leave the straightening out to chance.

SEX FACTS are better ABSORBED
when hidden FANTASIES
DO NOT STAND IN THE WAY.

What you do now isn't really too hard. Just remember about the dresses.

Bring out the old. Set it beside the new. Then the old and the new can be seen in contrast side by side.

Begin in your most comfortable and simple language. (In Part Four you'll find some "stories" to start you off, should you want them.) The important point is to say it in the way it's easiest for you. Perhaps the way you've thought of it will go like this: "The baby grew inside the mommy's tummy." That's the way most of us think to say it. And that's perfectly all right. But go on then. Instead of stopping and leaving it to the child's imagination, show which stomach you mean. Make it clear that you are talking of the whole front wall—the abdomen. "You grew inside here!" making a curving gesture to show where.

"But when you were inside the mommy, you were not in the mother's eating-stomach—not in the food-stomach—not in the stomach where the food goes." Just saying "the baby was in a special place," without mentioning where the baby was *not,* doesn't do it. The old fantasy needs to be laid out to be seen. And now for the new fact to place by its side. "You were in a special place: a place where only babies grow!"

"Oh," says Jean, "Oh!" her face radiant. "Oh, in a baby-growing room!"

With thanks to Jean, we can borrow her phrase. "You were in a special place for the baby—a baby-growing room inside the mother's body" or "inside the mother" or "inside the mother's tummy"—or any way you care to phrase it. You can

95

add, if you wish, "In her uterus, that's its grown-up name." But don't worry about the words too much. (See Story I, Part Four, p. 227.)

After all, children are used to having one word mean several things. "Through," for instance, means "through a door" or "I'm finished," or "threw," "I tossed a ball." Children get it straight readily enough because it isn't associated poignantly or nostalgically with old feelings and fantasies.

As long as we help a child take care of the old feelings and fantasies and compare the old false ideas with the new true facts, the words which are most comfortable will, as we said earlier, do the best job.

Paul shows, for example, that he has gotten the facts quite straight as he talks in his own words about the baby kittens he has discovered.

"I found them last night, the new kittens
In a box in the woodshed all curled into a round.
I saw their little glisteny eyes.

Before they were in the box
They were in the mother's stomach—
In the baby stomach;
Not in the pocket where the food is
But in another pocket near it."

And dreamily he runs on into feelings that belong universally to little creatures newly born:

"When they came out
My goodness, they took fast to sucking.
They love it all snuggling.
But when their mother pulled away
They cried, 'Meiw, meiw!' little and whiney
And they spit, 'Wihhu!'

And they closed their jaws
And let out their claws
Like they were mad
And wanted to scratch
And bite!"

And his mother, listening, wondered: "How much of what he is telling is about kittens? And how much is about him?"

8 | The Training Period and Sex

We have seen how in the first months of life, when a baby is small and helpless, all that he gets must be given him. We have seen how the power to receive and accept love, so important to eventual sexual adjustment, starts here.

The power to *give love* is equally important to mature sexual expression. The beginnings of this have their roots in those months when a child ordinarily is being "trained."

It seems a big jump from toilet training to sex and love. And it is a big jump. To understand it we must get the small child's point of view. There are not only years between us that separate us. There are thick layers of acquired propriety and prohibitions that make it almost painful to let our own imaginations carry us into seeing how it is to be a child.

With this in mind, let's go to *sex as a giving of self*.

A gift can be many different kinds of thing. In its best and finest sense, a gift is like "a part of me that comes to you with love."

In his imagination, as we shall see, a child's first gifts are part of him.

The First Gifts a Child Gives

The day comes when a baby no longer lies in his crib and simply eats, sleeps, and waits to be given to. He begins to navigate. In safe sight of his mother, or feeling himself at not too far a distance, he begins to follow his own small pursuits. He wanders to a pebbly path and scoops up handfuls of white shiny bits and watches them fall in a shower from his fists. He bangs a tin lid against another tin lid in noisy enjoyment. He picks up a snail from the grass. These are his treasures. And joyously he comes to his mother, his hand stretching to hers: Here is a white stone. Here a tin lid. Here a beautiful snail. With his discovery and his appropriation of it, it is *his*.

"Thank you," his mother says for the white stone. "Thank you," for the pot cover. But to his great and chagrined bewilderment, "Ugh!" she says. "That awful snail. Ugh! Put it down."

One gift is "good"; another isn't. A child must learn this very gradually. When he is small he has no discrimination. Moreover, he likes the feel of things that are moist and soft.

Momentarily he is hurt and angry. But the snail doesn't count for long. A snail is a matter of one occasion; not a constantly repeated event in his life. Not too close a part of himself. He didn't make it. He didn't produce it. He just picked it up from the ground.

But there are things that he does make and these do count. They are far more important, far more constantly with him. They are of daily concern. His mother herself has placed a great deal of emphasis on them. Of this he has become increasingly conscious in the months that have passed.

His mother has begun training him. She has taken him into the bathroom every so often and has repeatedly urged, "Do it, darling. Do it for Mommy!" And if his accomplishment has been too scanty she has asked him to "make some more."

And so it gradually dawns on him: "This is something my mother wants me to make for her."

He notices in his unabashed fashion that it comes from his body. In a primitive way he imagines that because of this, it is actually a part of him. It is his own product, an important gift from him to her.

Denny, with complete lack of embarrassment, sits on his pottie, his knees apart, watching what is happening. When he is through, he picks up the pot and, strutting proudly, carries it to his mother. "Me! Mine! I bringed it for you," he beams. He is not quite sure of his words. But that this is *his* possession he is sure. He has made it. And he offers it to his mother as a prize of great worth.

Ed, who is three, shows that the prizing of such gifts may transfer itself to other presents. He plays with clay. He rolls it out into a pile of chubby bits. He is making chocolates, he says. "Chocolates for Mommy. A present-full. A box-full. A pottie-full of chocolate poochies," with a wide and beatific smile.

When a child is little, another thing that makes him attach value to the products of his body is the fact that he gets pleasurable body-feelings in producing them.

To see this, let's go back to life's beginnings. We need to remember that to the infant, touch sensations are of extreme importance. Anything wet and warm and soft and slippery is enjoyed. He relishes the feel of warm water, warm slithery soap, or the warm oil with which he is rubbed. And he loves his mother's hands rubbing him and cleaning him off.

Torrie, three, watches his mother change the baby, and wistfully murmurs, "I don't get her so soft any more." Then he runs outside and "quite by accident" stumbles into a mud puddle and comes in to be changed. As his mother sponges and lathers him, he beams at her, crowing, "*I* got the soft-soaping now."

To the small child, feces and urine done in the diaper are warm and moist also. "No toilet!" protests a verbal two-year-old. "Why, darling?" "No, no, Mommy. It makes my tooshy too cold."

Moreover, as a small child voids when and where he wishes, there is no need for the discomfort of delay. He gains body pleasure connected with the relief and release from neuromuscular pressures without any intermediate period of holding back in uneasiness or pain.

Witness twenty-month-old Ted with his dog, George, in the yard.

"Higeorge," he says. "Comear!"

But George is otherwise occupied.

Ted stops in his tracks, fascinated. "Gotoi-toi? George go-to-john outside."

Pause. Hand on rear. "Gottago . . . I wet now. Gooboy dirty-too."

Since nature has equipped him with no sense of disgust or "dirtiness," he may use the word "dirty," but to him its meaning is different than to us. As did Ted, he oftener than not applauds himself for it. Even the odor fails to arouse revulsion. Many young children do, in fact, speak of the enjoyment they derive from these smells.

Linda, four, had gotten into her mother's row of cosmetic jars and had sniffed them experimentally one after another. "And what do you know?" her mother recounted. "The one with the most hideous odor, that was the one she liked the best. 'It's just like doggie's poohs,' she said."

To complicate the picture further, even though his mother may praise her child for his accomplishment, she flushes it down the toilet. To some children what has been "good" now seems "bad." Otherwise, why would Mother get rid of this gift? "Don't flush! Don't flush!" two-year-old Rheba repeats in tears.

"Why is she so frightened?" her mother asks.

"Because she imagines that a part of her is being drowned."

"Oh no! She can't! That's too fantastic!"

But one day Rheba's mother comes in and finds Rheba leaning over the toilet bowl, her arms in as far as they can reach. "I wanna find my bottie!" Rheba explains.

"But none of your bottom's in there!"

"All my gone botties is."

When children flush the toilet for themselves or help to do it, this fear can often be lessened. They love then to "watch the poochies dance and go round and slip into the tunnel." They get a sense that they themselves have done this, rather than that something has been taken away.

Enemas, particularly, make a child feel that something is being taken from him.

Rhoda, a young married woman whose mother had habitually given her enemas, could not respond in sexual intercourse. "I get panicky," she said. "I can't stand the thought of anything going into me. It makes me feel something terrible will happen. I'm going to lose my life or a part of myself."

Rectal thermometers at this stage of development can create fear-fantasies that are somewhat akin.

His mother notices that three-year-old Larry's wetting would increase each time he'd had a rectal temperature taken. And then, in his own words, Larry showed why. "When my temperature gets taken it makes me afraid. Afraid something more of me will be hurt." Unconsciously his hand covers his penis in a protecting gesture. "It makes me mad. Very mad. It makes me scared. Very scared!" And then one night, after wetting his bed, he pointed to the flood he had made and said, "See, I'm all right! See, I *can* wet."

In other words, Larry had to wet to prove to himself that he had not been injured. It was as if, in his imagination, along with what had been done behind him, his penis had somehow been hurt.

Spankings, too, are sometimes thought of as crippling. "I get so scared it will hurt my doodoo-maker and I won't be able to make my big-jobs any more. And sometimes I think the hurt might go all the way through me to my front."

Spankings do another thing that is worth considering from

the point of view of sex education. A child is spanked and for-
given. The spanking has expiated him. He feels his parents have
reinstated him in their affection. If this is repeated often, he may
come to use suffering as a means of getting love.

"I can't understand my wife," says a husband. "The only way
she ever seems happy is when I'm lambasting her. She goes after
it. It's as if she liked nothing better than for me to make her
into a nothing and to flatten her out."

By courting fights that lead to forgiveness the grown-up child
recreates the spanking–love-scenes he has failed to leave emotionally behind.

Giving Versus Giving Up

During this training period, the child's primary attachment
is still to his mother. He is still defenselessly dependent on her.
But, whereas he has been like a part of her before, he is now
starting to feel himself apart. Able, if he is healthy, to remove
himself into explorative short bursts of independence. To gain
a sense of being capable of achieving on his own.

Whereas before he may have been constantly cuddly, he now
is often a jumper-downer off laps. He is a runner-arounder. A
"getter." A go-getter.

He sees something on the coffee table. He dashes. Reaches.
Picks it up. He touches. Pokes. And drops. He is busy and bus-
tling. Self-starting. Self-propelling. Attempting to be self-run-
ning.

"And how he does love to run himself!"

"No!" and *"No!"* and again *"No!"* he says. Perpetually,
"No." Which is like saying, "To find that I can go *my* way, I
must turn down yours."

Clumsily he has little discrimination.

We, too, are full of *"Nos."* Just as it is his first response, so it
is ours. We limit him, as indeed we must in some ways. But

sometimes we feel we must in too many. He is limited, too, by his height and reach, by gaps in his knowledge and comprehension, by lacks in muscle coordination and control.

And so, for his security, it is tremendously important for him to feel for a while that there is something all his own to manage completely as he wishes. To know he can, and not to feel that he is "bad" in doing it.

The day will arrive when he has achieved a sense of body steadiness. When he can run without stumbles or bumps. When he can climb onto chairs or jungle gym without hesitance and go up and down stairs without doubting. With the managing of himself in such ways, the complete spur-of-the-moment managing of himself in eliminating will become less essential to him. He will be readier then for "training," feeling what is most important in his sexual maturing—that he is *giving* rather than *giving up*.

And so we can see—

How we handle toilet training is important in sex education.

"Training" Needs and Deeds

Haste is waste: We know it's wise to wait until comprehension of what's expected, interest, and the will to do are ready for teamwork. We know that muscles and nerves must be ready, too, to follow *with ease* what is attempted or else so much strain invades the accomplishment that fear of failure and anger shove out the sense of successful achievement.

All told, we realize today that it's not wise to start bowel training until around a year of age or later if freedom in body coordinations is not well established. We know also that it's best to let training for urinary control rest until around a child's second birthday, and even then to expect occasional accidents until around four years of age.

Pressures oppress: We know further that when training is not pressed, a child gets a firmer sense of accomplishment. If he seems to object, stopping and waiting is the best plan. Maybe picking it up again a week or two later does better than forcing the issue at the time.

Ignoring is not good either: However, we have sometimes mistaken letting up on too early or pressureful training to mean: Let it be; don't train at all. He'll train himself.

One couple following this policy, for instance, left their boy entirely to his own devices. At four years the child was ill and the doctor inquired how his bowels were functioning. The mother with an insulted gesture and the father with pride avowed that they never inquired. The child's bowels were his affair.

At thirteen, the boy was caught robbing newspaper collection boxes on the various street corners of the town. When his father with dignity assured him that despite his misdeeds his mother and he still loved him, the boy looked at him, disbelieving. Turning his face aside, he remarked, "Oh yeah! Except when I'm crummy. Why, you couldn't even look at my b.m.'s when I was small."

At thirty, another "boy" still wants his crummy parts accepted. "He never showers," his wife complains. "He drops things all over. He makes little piles of ashes on every table, strews piles of clothes on the floor and leaves piles of crumpled newspapers in his bed. . . ."

When a child has been given plenty of time but continues soiling or wetting, then perhaps we can ask ourselves: Have we let him know clearly enough what we do and do not approve of? It's time now for us to say, "Look, that was all right when you were a baby. You'd like to keep on being messy and wet. It feels good in your panties" (accepting the feelings). "But" with very serious and kindly firmness, "we don't like you to do it there any more" (clearly indicating unacceptable acts).

Finding acceptable channels: As we see, then, during this

time of life a child wants to give his gifts to his mother. He wants also to continue the messing enjoyments.

How can we help him channel these normal messing desires into acceptable acts? How let him get acceptable satisfactions to lessen the sense of frustration that toilet training usually brings? How prevent the rigid holding back on unfinished urges which often leads into constrictions in sex?

What to mess with to live out this urge?

Mud puddles in which to slosh in the rain. A moist earth-hole to dig in when the warm days come, or to sit in "all bare" if he wants. Sand is too gritty for this purpose! As Betty put it, "Sand's sharpish with pebblies; mud's smoothish with guish."

"My Judd," one mother reported, "sat in his private mud puddle for a solid hour blinking like a lizard in the sun. And that night, believe it or not, he didn't soil his bed!"

Moist clay is good, too, the kind that is water soluble. (This can be bought at most art stores. Ask for Sculptor's Clay. It may be had in powdered form to be mixed with water, or already mixed; and it can be kept from drying out by storing it in a plastic bag.) Endless possibilities come also when flour, salt, and water are kneaded into a pliable mass. One mother adds some drops of vegetable coloring and her little girl carries the flour-clay with her from morning till night, making bumps and lumps and "mustaches that stick" and long and short "snake things" with great relish.

And water and water and more water is wanted. Some leisurely bath times. A washtub out in the sunshine filled with water to splash in. A running sprinkler turned low. A hose with a small, slow stream. A plastic oven-baster and a bowl of soap-suds. ("Oh!" with glee from Leila, listening to the sound as she presses and releases the bulb. "Oh! It does fanny-talk too.")

All such soft and moist messing delights during the training period make other delights easier then and after.

And as for the giving of gifts to Mother, the possibilities are endless. But first and foremost, Mother must take time to sit down on occasion and turn as focused attention on new, more growing-up offerings as she did on the original baby-thing. Her appreciation of mud pies handed to her, of a bowlful of clay "wormsers" or "bees" or "buttons," or her admiration of a

Patsy, chanting:

"Know I like wet so well?
What a deal!
Real real wet!
Oh I just love everyone.
I'm so glad
'Cause I'm so glad
With wet."

beautifully messy finger-painting will help her child progress in his sexual development.

As time passes, she can offer opportunities for less messy gifts. Handing her silver from a tray as she sets the table: "Thank you for that spoon; thank you for that fork!" (At this age, handing means giving from-me-to-you.) Picking up a

"Shirt, please" and a "tablecloth next" and "another shirt, dear" and putting them into the hamper or washing machine with: "You did it for Mommy!" Admiring a block piled on another block: "You made that all by yourself!" Such commendations gradually raise the level of what a child makes and does for another person and of what he gives of himself.

If all goes fairly well during the training period, and if a mother is able to be natural and earthy and easy with a child in his primitive functioning, honestly acceptant of his good feelings about it, but making it gradually, gently, and firmly apparent that she does care about his learning to control his actions, he is more apt to feel that what he produces can be given proudly and with affection. But at one and the same time the idea is planted that as he grows his love gifts are not to be dropped indiscriminately all over the place.

Toilet Bonds and Bombs

We think we're supposed to avoid displeasure over a child's failures.

We think we're supposed never, never, never to wrinkle up our noses or give any looks of disgust.

But, probably nine chances out of ten, we ourselves were pressed when we were small. There was too great stress on being clean too early. Many feelings connected with elimination were marked taboo and were never talked of. They were shut inside. Out of our sight and out of our conscious control. As result, many of us never learned to really control our bowels. Many of us with persistent constipation or colitis find that our bowels still control us.

Fears connected with bowel control can even reach into the sexual act. Yolanda, for instance, is tense and nervous in sex relations. "I seem to be holding on so tight, I can't relax and let go."

She remembered that in childhood she had been punished

severely for "accidents." She remembered, too, that even as a child she had gotten "jittery" and that at such moments a phrase would habitually slip into her mind: "Now Yoli, hold on tight." She didn't recall, however, where the sentence had originated.

And then one day she recaptured a childhood scene. "I was playing in the garden and I called to my mother that I had to go. She rushed out, her forehead as wrinkled with wrath and worry as a turtle's neck. Something terrible will happen if you let go." And, hesitantly, "Could it be that I got sex mixed up with elimination and think the same thing could happen if I let go now?"

Unconsciously this sort of mix-up had come.

When we approach the matter of teaching toilet control to our children, there are all sorts of feelings that may push in and possess us.

Perhaps unconsciously we are still secretly wishing we might live out what we originally were taught to believe was "bad"— our own unmentionable and primitive interest in the eliminative processes. Perhaps our original failures to meet almost impossible expectations in regard to cleanliness made us feel so unloved that we now turn to our children to love us more. Then the close and intimate situation of toilet training may offer a welcome way of prolonging the bond.

To our children, this is welcome too. As a five-year-old puts it, "We have very much fun. . . . The phone rings and my mother says, 'I gotta go' and I say, 'I gotta go' and she chooses me over the phone."

An advanced child of seven writes a story about a little boy (himself really) who wouldn't get clean. His mother, he comments, couldn't do anything about it,

> "So she ket rigth on wiping and rubing, making him fell good. That was his way of having his mother privet."

"I didn't wipe myself," said a man, "until I was twelve. It was my way of keeping my mother, of taking her from my stepfather and the other kids. I'd trail after her like I trail after my wife now and take her from the children, much to her annoyance. Just like a child who'll explode if he isn't attended to at once."

But regardless of how much a child on the one hand may welcome such a bond with mother, on the other hand he resents it. For no matter how deeply it is hidden, the need to become one's own self—an independent being—is violated. And the individual is bound to protest.

More often, however, than creating such a bond through toilet training, we unwittingly create battles. Again our own training probably plays its part. Perhaps remnants of overstrictness which made us disgusted with ourselves when we were, or wanted to be, messy make us overstrict or disgusted with our children now. This adds to a child's sense of frustration in life as he lives it during inevitably frustration-full days.

Whether or not he shows anger forthrightly, most every child is angry many times during this period. Over many things. At his own ineptness, failures, weaknesses. At life's new demands. (It is always hard to give up old pleasures.) Even though he wants to please us, he still resents us and our wishes which are the reverse so often of his. Anger from infancy may be carried over, too.

And so—

What at some moments are gifts, at other moments are warlike missiles.

A child may unconsciously hold in to fight his parents, letting his constipation get even for him by causing them worry. He may hold in, too, to keep from letting out what he imagines to be a stream of violence. He may let out and soil or wet as ways of doing battle for him. Or he may use diarrhea unconsciously to get his parents down.

Consciously also children when angry think of excretions as weapons.

110

"Doodoo bombs!" shouts four-year-old Carl, "a whole airplane-full. Pffftzzz! down they come," with appropriate sounds. "Pttrwtt, prrwtt, prrwt—out of my machine gun too."

In more sophisticated fashion, Nate, six, wistfully confides:

"I wish I were a bird
'Cause birds can fly
Over people they're mad at
And do what they want
Right down on them.
And fly away fast then
And not get caught."

Urine, too, may become "poison water!"

"I will shoot you with my poison water and you'll shrivel and die," says eight-year-old Royce to his younger sister.

"I'll gas you up with my stink-bomb-maker," the not-to-be-daunted six-year-old retorts.

Some children want to fill themselves full with such ammunition. As one youngster put it, "I'll have such a bellyful of stink-bombs and poison gas that my explosions will explode the world." But this is frightening, too. "Oh goodness!" with a sudden gasp, "I'll explode *me*."

Such imaginings and others concerned with a sense of fullness, with explosions, and bursting, hitch up later with the concepts that a child forms about birth. It leads into the fantasy of the mother's body bursting open when a baby is born.

But far more important are the emotional undercurrents that may run from infancy into adulthood. The baby smears his bed. The three-year-old mutters, "You old pooh" when he is angry. The teen-ager grunts, "He's a mess!" or "She's a drip!" And the adult who is angry underneath may spend a lifetime joining smear campaigns or "griping" (a bowel term also) at husband or wife.

Sex Education for Remnants
Untrained and Untamed

What a Body Makes

So far as sexual adjustment and love are concerned, one of the great burdens of our culture is that our bodies and what our bodies create are considered "messy." The gift and the giving part are too often buried and lost.

What comes out of the body is thought of as "dirty." The proximity of the sexual organs and organs of elimination add to confusion. The body "down there," if wet or moist, is "dirty." Excessive or exaggerated fear of "germs" that will carry something hurtful from one body to another is just one remnant of the fantasy that such "dirtiness" will do harm.

It is easy to see that—

Imaginings from the training period associated with elimination may travel to the closely located sexual organs.

Patsy, seven, has discovered that she can get good feelings by touching herself. But then she grows frightened. "I'm so moisty I must be all germy. I gotta not touch." (Whatever one's opinion happens to be on masturbation—and we'll come to this later —one can gather from what we are saying here that threatening with "dirt" or "germs" is not a healthy deterrent. It only confirms the child's own fears.)

"When I marry, my husband won't want ever to come near

me," a teen-age girl shamefully laments. "I've got some sickness. And I wonder, too, if it'll keep from me from having babies?" What she is referring to is the fluid that normally flows from the vagina from time to time, especially before and after the menstrual period and when sexual feelings are aroused.

A preadolescent boy worriedly wonders, "How can a girl stand your being so dirty and going to the toilet into her?" With many youngsters, not only does the sex act become confused with urination, but both acquire an imaginary tinge of "dirt."

The anus and vagina are often thought of as one and the same opening by both boys and girls. "What!" says an eight-year-old boy on learning about intercourse. "You mean a daddy puts his penis in the b.m. place? Well, being a daddy is not for me."

And yet when people get married, suddenly certain parts of the body and the products closely located to these "dirty" areas are supposed to be cleanly related to wholesome loving.

Semen is clean. Moisture in the vagina is desirable during excitation. The vagina itself—so often confused with the anus, or rectum—is clean.

But in the secret, hidden, unconscious thoughts, the hostile and dirty meanings may remain. They may invade the sexual sphere. The sexual act then becomes a dirty act or a contaminating or injuring act. And various sexual difficulties ensue.

In many bedrooms, after the shades are down and the lights are turned off, a shameful act is performed in the dark, quickly and mechanically to hide, for one thing, that the childish imaginings which unconsciously linger still divorce it from love that is "clean."

A child learns slowly that the products he prizes so highly are not really a valuable part of himself but waste food or fluid. Gradually he learns that he can make more valuable gifts. He paints a picture. Fashions a paperweight. And later builds bookshelves or knits a sweater, depending on his sex. And still later gives of himself in a smile that is cherishing, in attentive listening, in active contributing, in merging embrace. But the spirit of those first giving of gifts sometimes prevails.

If a child has felt he was "good" in producing them, he is more apt not only to feel proud of his future productions but to feel also that he is "good" in making them and in being the kind of person who can. If he was angry and has not wanted to give, he may stay "stingy" and hold back. Or if he has felt that his more intimate gifts, like the snails, were disgusting, then he may feel disgust with himself, with his body and with whatever it is and does.

"I can't write decently," for example. "It looks all crummy!" ... "I can't look decent." ... "Whatever I do, it's messy. I myself am nothing but a terrible mess."

These feelings are more widespread than we commonly suspect.

And so we ask:

What can we do after the training period is past to help a child take care of the remnants that may interfere with sex and loving later on?

We will recall that—

FEELINGS and fantasies
GOTTEN OUT EVEN BELATEDLY
through nonhurtful channels
can
REDUCE HURTS.

Two questions are particularly productive in handling leftovers from this period:

How shall we help our children get out unfinished messing pleasure belatedly to reduce its pull? And how help them steer and control their hostile wishes to do dirt?

114

As we keep our weather eye out for signs of emotional remnants, perhaps we will see as we never saw before how the messing business invades the scene. Perhaps we will find in our homes and schoolrooms unsuspected signals for help.

Says father to mother: "Laura, this kid is impossible. Look at his desk. Have you ever seen such accumulated crud?"

So there it is.

It goes against you to have desks littered. But perhaps a litter-box in the garage or a special shelf or drawer signed "messily yours" may help to steer the messing into more acceptable channels.

Meanwhile, "I know, there's a kind of easy satisfaction in being messy. I used to be that way too." Perhaps also admitting: "When children are small, they enjoy being messy and I never gave you your proper chance!" This may strike a little tune that is merrily welcome. For it tells a child that some of the things that originally made him feel "bad" weren't so bad after all. It may make him more willing, too, to meet your limits now when you add, "But still we cannot have messes all over the house."

As for legitimate channeling of the messing urge: collections and hobbies can serve useful ends here. In some cases, they may prove to be "just so much rubbish" to be discarded as the child grows. In other cases they may grow with him into something of material value. In either event, one of their very important emotional values lies in helping a child steer his interest in "junk."

Clothes that can be gotten messy help, too. And so do materials with which one can mess. To have these at hand, not only during the training period (as already suggested), but all through childhood, is a good idea. The end-products may or

115

may not become more symmetrical and shapely with the passing of years. But the manipulative joy and the "feel" of the material still holds its own worth. So again: Damp clay. Paints and the like. And, if possible, a place where they can be used as one wishes—"sloppily," says Erna, "not fussily."

In a kindergarten room, Mrs. Sprague knows that children of four and five normally carry over from two and three a need to work out their enjoyment of messing and wetting. And so in one corner of the room she has a linoleum rug, and on it a dishpan of clay and a pitcher of water. Two girls now are in it up to their elbows, pouring and "mix-messing" with giggles of delight. A short while ago the dishpan had been the target in a battlefield and one of the boys had flung clay bombs vigorously down onto it. Yesterday it was a mud hole, and the day before just "slish."

Meanwhile, when the hour for cleaning up draws near, plenty of time is allowed. "It's more fun to dribble water, squeezing the sponge again and again, than it is to mop the linoleum dry," says the teacher. "But we manage that, too, in the end."

In another kindergarten there is a play toilet in the doll house corner and baby dolls to "spank" and change, who invariably "get wet again."

The Problem of "Dirty Talk"

Sooner or later it's natural for the "dirty" remnants in children to come out in dirty talk. As one child said, "Babies have their throw-ups and their bee-ems for weapons. They have good ammunition, better than skunks. Bigger boys have words."

Duffy, five-and-a-half, illustrates this.

When I'm mad,
I can't throw rocks
I can't throw blocks or shoes or bombs or poochies.
But I can throw words—
When I'm alone with you—

116

Poison words—
Like Stinky! Pooh-face!
Tinkle-face!
Icky!
Pee-pot!
Stinky-Pop!
Be quiet you,
    You big dumb pooh.

At five-and-a-half the words may take this form. Later they take on four-letter spelling of more notorious fame.

"Oh shit!" says an eight-year-old at the dinner table. Looks up and catches his older sister's horrified expression. Quickly, "I meant to say 'Oh shoot'! But that's the way it came out."

"Okay, okay!" says his father. "It slipped out purposely by accident, I would guess. Next time better not. Not around Mother or the girls. That's man-talk."

"Only for use with certain people and in certain places," says Sister with superiority. And then with a sly grin, "The same goes when it's used as girl-talk, too!"

"Some words are cruddy. Some are sexy," says an eighteen-year-old. "Used appropriately both are most expressive, I find."

How you handle this sort of thing will depend upon your own reactions and on how your youngster uses such words. You can pretty well tell whether he is talking this way to let out hostility or because four-letter words are the words that he best "likes the feel of" in referring to body parts or processes or to sex. Some children, as well as adults, use these words to take the place of earlier baby words. Some also use them to feel important.

An eleven-year-old explained it in his way, "They're not always mad words, Dad. They're words that make you feel big. When you say them, the kids like you better."

When a youngster uses such words to gain status with his friends, it's as if he were transforming into verbal products the physical products which he took much earlier to his first friend, his mother, as a gift to make her think well of him.

In similar fashion, later, he may use monosyllables in his love-making, not with any hostile connotations, but rather to put into his own intimate terms his gifts of love.

In any event, we will need, as with other things, to be honest about our own feelings.

One mother said, for instance, "I know you and some of the children use those words. I don't like them myself. And I'd definitely prefer it if you didn't when I'm around."

If we fuss and make a great to-do about them, however, instead of realizing that in our culture this is a common way of channeling old wishes, we revive the earlier battle over training. By arguments thrown back and forth, a youngster gets back his mother's attention and throws his bombs at her once again.

Again, we do better if we can take the child's feelings more specifically into account.

A wonderful sixth-grade teacher realizes that dirty words are bound to come into her classroom. "And so," she says, "when I find a sheet scrawled with them, I say—trying to identify the children's feelings—'Someone's had a wonderfully messy or angry time and felt very big and important this way!' We talk about using these words. They discuss why they like to use them. (The feeling part.) But we also limit their usage. (The action part.) 'They're best marked 'taboo in here'."

In addition, providing other outlets for the wish to feel big, other outlets for hostile feelings, other outlets for giving, reduces the need to use such words on and on.

Ideas that Need Cleaning Up

In essence: From feelings and fantasies common during the training period, children commonly get certain mixed-up ideas about sex.

If we understand these, when the proper time comes we can

118

help our children differentiate between fact and fiction. We need to help them differentiate, for one thing, between the organs and functions of elimination and the organs and functions of sex.

When we talk about birth we will help them see that it is not an exploding or bursting process.

When they seek understandings about impregnation and birth, we will help them to know that the anus and the vagina are two separate openings. And that semen and urine are two separate fluids.

As we observe children at various periods of their development, we may observe remnants, too, of the earlier idea that feces were an actual part of the body. And this, too, we will help them get straight.

Usually, discussions of these matters have more meaning to children after they have begun to notice anatomical differences between the sexes, as when brothers or sisters are on the way or are born, or when little friends are more intimately encountered. (We will therefore take them up a little later.)

Meanwhile, letting the old feelings come out as we have indicated relieves pressure. Then the child no longer needs to cling so hard to his beliefs in fantasy to resolve his hates and fears and loves. He grows more ready to accept sex realistically as he matures.

10 | Noticing Anatomical Differences

During the training period, with interest in the body's productions high, the child's interest in the body itself also mounts and continues over the ensuing years.

I Notice Me

Small children point with pride to parts of their bodies and enjoy naming them. "Eyes" ... "Nose" ... "Mouth" ... "Toes." Some children go on—down and up—unembarrassed. They gayly include: "Toto" and "Tinkler" or whatever their terms are.

Many children, before they have grown very old, catch the fact that there is more privacy due certain areas. "The upper parts over the pants, those are okay, Evvie. But the parts under the pants, those you only talk about in private," big sister cautions her small sister sternly.

There are other forbiddings, too. The main one: *"Don't touch!"*

For the little boy, learning about himself is simpler than for the little girl. The parts he is most curious about are out in the open. Even the proper names are more commonly spoken. "That's your penis, Tommy. Your pee-nis. It's easy to say" (and to see).

120

"And this here?"

"Lots of people call that 'the balls.' But the grown-up word is 'testicles.' That's a bit harder."

Some little girls learn to identify the triangle between their legs as the "vulva." You play as you help your daughter bathe, perhaps—"Now we scrub your knees, now we wash higher up your legs and your vulva."

"Bulba?" asks Sue.

"Try again, darling. 'Vulva'—that's the word."

But the matter does not end here. Most little girls are interested in what's between the folds of pink flesh.

"The vagina's there," we may tell them. But if they explore, trying to locate just where the vagina is, most of us—remembering our own training—recoil.

Nor does the matter end even here.

"What's it?" asks Sue, still insistent, pointing to the little raised place near the front.

"That's the clitoris."

"It's the best-feeling place," says Sue, unembarrassed.

"At which point," confesses Sue's mother, "I folded."

But Sue, all undaunted, still wanted to know, "Where does the wee come out?" She sees it clearly on her brother but is puzzled about herself.

Words are one thing. We can explain, "There's a little hole or opening called the urethra right below the clitoris. Up in front of the vagina." But it's still hard to actually see it, even if one is an agile small contortionist. Certainly with our feelings about the body parts mentioned, we do not want to be part to examining. (And we know now that in any case it's best not to be.) However, the old ideas implanted in us long ago usually still make us want to caution: Let it rest. Don't explore. Or, in simplest terms: "Don't touch."

But children do explore. They do touch. Both boys and girls discover gradually and normally where the "best-feeling" spots

121

are. And normally, they continue to seek these good feelings through touching.

This serves a purpose in their development and progress toward growing up. It helps them move their most pleasurable focus toward the portions of the body involved in adult, mature sexuality.

In other words—

It is part of healthy maturing for children to discover and settle on the fact that their most pleasurable sensations come from their genitals.

Says a child of six, "My rear end used to be the most interesting. Now my front end is." And this movement forward is healthy.

Settling Where the Best Feelings Are

At this point, however, most of us come up against our own ancient anxieties. Perhaps we heard some of the old wives' tales about how masturbation could destroy normal sex life, make childbearing impossible, cripple one in some way or make one go crazy. Perhaps we felt we were already on the downward journey because in adolescence we couldn't stop. As one man put it, "In my teens I tried awfully hard not to masturbate. I held agonized conversations with myself not to. My mother had said I'd go crazy. . . . And I thought I must be weak in the head already because no matter how sternly I'd forbid myself, I'd always end by doing it again." Perhaps we were told it was "just a nasty habit" or that it would "make us sore down there." The implication was the same. This was something one had to stop. Perhaps nothing at all was said but we discerned the general attitude of disapproval that prevailed.

And so in our children it's often hard to see that masturbation isn't wrong. It's hard to realize that most children touch themselves normally, that they get good body-feelings from doing so. It's hard for some of us even to accept the fact that no physical harm can come from masturbation, although medical and psychological science has by now proved this beyond a doubt. The harm comes when fear and anxiety concerning masturbation grow too intense.

If a child masturbates continuously, if he chooses it in preference to playing as other children do, then we can begin to think of it as an indication that he is perhaps not as emotionally at peace as he should be. Perhaps he is using masturbation as a retreat because in some way life seems too hard for him. Then getting at what makes life too hard is the needed approach. Perhaps he is using masturbation as a hostile gesture. "I know I can get them to squirming and looking uncomfortable if I touch my teetee while I'm watching TV," six-year-old Zelda confided to the psychologist. "Then I'm more important even than the best glamour person on the screen."

When a child must masturbate to feel more important than the hero or heroine on the program, other feelings are obviously involved—jealousies possibly which touch closer home, as jealousy of a more glamorous mother, for example. Then, for one thing, other means of discharging hostility are called for (as we know by now).

In any event, when masturbation becomes either a constant means of retreat or an embarrassingly open and defiant gesture, it should be taken as one piece of evidence in a larger picture indicating that professional help might wisely be sought.

In the normal course of development, however, we can expect a child to masturbate. Even when we do not ourselves disapprove, he may run into disapproval elsewhere. Through innuendoes and gossip if nothing else. So, if we can, it's wise before this happens to bring the matter out into the open and to get it as straight as possible.

Five-year-old Trina's father and mother did this after they noticed their little daughter one day on the beach running down again and again to the water's edge. Squatting, spread-leggedy

123

low. Waiting. Waiting entranced for a little wave to come and lap over her between her thighs. Then jumping up and clapping her hands and squealing, "It kissed me. It kissed me!" And squatting some more.

In the car going home they noticed also that Trina was fingering herself.

"Cause it feels good like the waves kissing you?" Trina's mother wondered aloud.

"Uhuh," said Trina.

"We know it feels good," said Trina's father.

Then taking Trina comfortably in her lap, Mother talked further while Father approved. She brought out what many other parents have brought out helpfully in the sex education of their children.

These feelings do feel good.

"And they are feelings that people like to feel most when they are in bed. In fact, that's the best place to feel them."

Some parents can go along with this. Others can't. But perhaps they can do what ten-year-old Barry's father did. He included his own feelings, too, frankly knowing that this was better than putting on an air that was not sincere.

"I'm embarrassed as heck about this, Barry," he said. "When I was a child I was told stupidly that touching yourself there was harmful. Some people still think so and may frighten you by saying it does all kinds of awful things to you. But I've found out that's nonsense. It's perfectly normal and natural. And it doesn't do any harm. I thought I'd better tell you on account of having given you the wrong impression when you were little."

"Gee, Dad, you don't know how good it is to hear what you're saying. I hated you so at times for having scared me. But I like you like anything now."

Seeing Adults

In the days when sex education was focused on bringing ideas out of the tight-laced corsets of still earlier days, we preached

124

the gospel of untrammeled freedom. "So long as parents are comfortable, free, and easy," we said, "let children be around freely when parents are undressed. This will help the children feel more comfortable and easy themselves." But it didn't.

Gradually we learned that children are apt to be more bothered than freed. Seeing adult bodies in the nude without any barriers can bring in fear-fantasies that are harder to handle than any of the imaginings that arise out of seeing bodies of one's own size. The very bigness of father and mother combined with the bigness of children's feelings toward father and mother may make too great intimacy too overpowering.

We can understand this point better if we realize that when the child's body sensitivities are becoming focused normally on the genital area, their attachments are still focused strongly on their parents. Their parents are still the objects of their deepest desire for intimacy.

Seeing parents' bodies now makes for a new set of problems. To be more specific, in infancy when the focus of body sensitivities had so much to do with mouth-feelings, the sight or smell or feel of mother's breast could stimulate the baby's mouth responses, which in turn involved the whole of him. Similarly now, when the child's focus has begun to move to the genitals, the sight of the big people with whom he most craves intimacy can be stimulating to this area. But, whereas the stimulation of mouth-feelings earlier led to contacts with the mother's body suitable for that age and stage, the stimulation of genital feelings cannot lead to any suitable contacts. Whereas the earlier mouth stimulation brought on feelings that were appropriate and could end with appropriate satisfactions, the stimulating experiences now bring on feelings that are inappropriate and must be denied.

And yet, quite naturally, children are curious. They want to see.

At the breakfast table Dennis, seven, tells of a dream he had during the night. "In the dream it was moonlight as bright as day and Daddy came in to talk to me."

"What did he have on?" His five-year-old sister interrupts.

"Oh," says Dennis, "pajama tops."

"Not the pants?"

"No, just the tops."

"You, Denny! That's not fair. You got to see him in your dream. You get all the good deals."

But when the pleasure of seeing is real rather than dreamed of, it is apt to generate more anxiety.

"When they're in their nakeds, I'm so curious," from another very observant seven-year-old boy. "My father's busts are flat fat. My mother has long busts sticking out. They look like pee-wee tubes on her chest. Women's breasts when they're older look like autumn leaves. Will my peewee get all flattened down like that?" (Notice the confusion between breasts and penises and the way the child refers the problem in his mind to himself.)

In nursery school, three-year-old Ron asks, "What do you call a tinkler on a Daddy?"

"A penis," the teacher answers factually.

"Oh," says Ron, his eyes wide. "But my Daddy doesn't have a peanut. He's got a baseball bat."

At thirty, another Ronald still feels that his perfectly normal organ is abnormally small. "You should have seen my father's," he says. In spite of reality, he still carries over anxiety concerning his sexual adequacy.

Obviously, however, in the course of the years and in the compactness of city apartments and homes, children are bound to see.

Perhaps, like Jeannette's mother, we have tried to keep "innocence sublime": "I really don't believe she ever, ever has seen anything!"

But one day, four-year-old Jeannette unexpectedly turned the handle of the bathroom door and started to open it after her father had gone in. Her mother rushed up excitedly.

126

Deliberately Jeannette pulled the door shut and, turning to her mother, said, "Don't you worry. It's all right. He was just putting it away."

A boy naturally goes to the men's room with his father. During earlier toilet-training days, seeing his father on occasion stand to urinate encourages him to do it like Daddy. In the course of play, or pushed by some immediate need, a child may happen to come in while parents are dressing. Such occasional occurrences may arouse curiosity, may arouse wonderings, may arouse some fear-fantasies, but these can be handled.

The occasional glimpse will not of itself leave lasting scars. But the child who gets such an occasional glimpse is having quite a different sort of experience from the child whose parents let him continuously see them bathe, sunbathe, exercise in the nude, or dress and undress.

When the latter situation prevails, a child often imagines he is being invited in. He is treated, as it were, on a level with the grown-ups, as an equal of these so much bigger people. Then especially does the stimulation prove too stimulating. And the child feels himself endangered, powerless and weak.

It's best if parents can *acknowledge a child's curiosity but maintain their own privacy.*

Four-year-old Ellie kept bursting into the bathroom whenever her father was showering. "I gotta have a Band-aid! I gotta have my toothbrush! I gotta get my pink soap!"

"Such a line of nonsense," her mother recounted. "We soon caught on.

"I hazarded, 'I think you want to see Daddy? Most little girls do!' And to my surprise, she spoke right up. 'I did see him once upon a time and I liked it. I want to some more. You're mean to make him lock the door.' So I reassured her that I knew how she felt but that Daddy and I had learned that parents need privacy. But I knew, too, that she naturally would feel mad at being shut out. . . ."

127

As we've said, most children in the ordinary course of events will have caught glimpses of father and mother and longer views of other children.

Some fear-fantasies will normally follow. We cannot prevent this. But we can help children handle them so that they do not grow too big. When given a chance to speak freely, most young children are eager to share what they've seen. In this manner they bring into the open the things that concern them.

In a kindergarten, for instance, the class is busily discussing the differences between men and women and boys and girls.

"Men have trousers," from a boy.

"Ladies do too," from a girl.

"Ladies have pony-tails, boys don't."

"Some people have bumps, some people haven't."

"Some have hair everywhere. Some have bald spots. And Daddies have businesses for to work at and for to use in the bathroom. . . . Both kinds!"

"And boys have those little tassle dangles that get all tangled up in their underpants," from a very positive little girl.

"My mother's got her penis kind of hidden. But she's got it," stoutly from a four-year-old boy who, like a lot of boys, is worried to see that a penis can be lacking on any body.

"I can't see my mother's. She got too many feathers covering it up."

"My mother's belly-button humps out. That's where she had a penis once but it got cut off."

"Even a cow," Milton insists, "has so many penises."

"All the sticky-out places," Fred, who is almost six, elaborates. "All the humps and bumps and sticky-out places, they make me feel good. The dumps and in-places don't."

From three-year-old Moira in nursery school, mauling the guinea pig, "I gotta find the guinea-peg's peg."

And from two-year-old Helen, who has an older brother, as she is sitting with her legs wide apart in the sunshine, the sprinkler splattering cool dots on her back, "What'sa matter with my 'gina? The tongue that sticks out got lost."

Is Something Lacking?

Hard though it is for parents to see this, both boys and girls normally do worry: Something is wrong.

An eight-year-old boy still struggling with his earlier feelings, writes a tale about a "Broken Buddem." In it he says, "I was afraid I wood be a girl."

A five-year-old watches his mother diapering his baby sister. "I don't like it," he says. "It makes me feel scarey when she lies there all opened up." His hand goes to his own crotch and clutches his penis. "Will mine come off too?"

Many little boys think: If it happened to her, it could happen to me.

Many little girls think: It did happen.

All of this may sound very strange to us. But it becomes clearer if we can realize that what a child notices at this stage in his development probably plays back on earlier fear-fantasies. In their moments of anger, as we will remember, with clamping mouth and clutching nails a baby may seem to say: "I want to bite and tear." The mirror image of this often is evidenced in a child later. He imagines as punishment: "I will be torn." (Says a seven-year-old, "You can just expect others to do unto you like you want to do unto them.") . . . Vague recollections of enemas, too, can enter: "What part of me was it that came out with that rush?"

When children notice bodily differences, some of these echoes from times past may resound in their minds and contribute to their fear-fantasies. (Almost universally in their imaginings, as we've seen, children tie anger, punishment, and hurt together.)

129

The caution "not to touch" may have added its threats. Moreover, the fact that this part of the body is normally developing the best feelings makes it most precious, so that fear of any injury very naturally focuses on it.

But there is something even bigger and more vital: the healthy need that we talked of earlier, to feel whole and "beautifully made."

**A person is helped
to get a sense of
WHAT HE HIMSELF IS
through
WHAT HE FEELS HIS BODY IS.**

Many of us experience a kind of sample of this in the increased ease that comes when we feel well-dressed or in the opposite feeling of discomfort and shyness that come when one looks like an "old hag."

Behind the clothes, what an individual feels about his body in childhood gives him a kind of basic image of self to live by. And this plays an important part in his sex life.

A young man who had been a handsome and stalwart child, in his teens got polio and lost the use of his legs. Yet, from his wheelchair, he would say, "I just walked to the store," or "I ran to the door." In his mind he was still stalwart and able. In contrast, a very glamorous young woman had felt herself the "ugly duckling" in the family as a child, "with a caved-in chest and a too-flat nose." This was the image that persisted in spite of being told she was "gorgeous" by admirers galore.

A sensitive child tells a story which gets at what is far more important to most normal children than the caved-in chest or the too-flat nose. "The little girl stood and looked down all the way at herself and said, 'Oh my, I look too plain. I don't like it!' She wanted to have what she didn't have because in the childhood stage a girl doesn't have anything that sticks out and is beautiful. Later she gets breasts that stick out and are beautiful, but not as a child. And she thinks life's unfair."

"I used to think I had a penis," says a little girl. "And that was a beautiful thought while it lasted."

If a child feels that any part of him has been injured, he wants poignantly to be able to reconstruct it and become whole and sound once more. If he—or she—thinks something is lacking, he wants desperately to mend the lack. If he feels that something may happen, he wants to avoid it at all costs.

All of this has particular application for the little girl even before she moves her emotional focus to her father. While she is still deeply attached to her mother, she notices her mother's focus on her father. She sees her mother, for instance, going to bed with him. And she notices, too, that her father has an organ she doesn't have. If she has brothers, she observes that they have it also and she may imagine that because they have "more" than she, not only has she been hurt, but mother loves them better. She is jealous. In her own small way in her own time of life, she wants to be top man, as it were, with mother. (A boy, too, can wish to be a girl, "to have a baby like Mother does" possibly, or to be like the sister he feels is preferred.)

For a variety of reasons, the little girl more frequently wants what she hasn't got. She may dream up all kinds of imaginary substitutes for the missing organ. "I got a long pony-tail instead," says one. "When I grow up I'll get long, long fingernails," says another. Says a third, "In my b.m. place I've got a lot of little brown brown hidden penises. If one goes out, another comes in. So you never, never have none." In one way or another the little girl may try to by-pass and avoid the fact of her lack.

She may try to stand up to urinate, for instance, as if she were unaware that she has no penis and as if she wanted one, all at the same moment.

"Boys can do it," says five-year-old Mimi resentfully. "Boys

131

are so irrigating!" she adds, her nose held high in disgust. "But I'll fool my brother yet. I'll go in and sneak his off him sometime when he's asleep."

If the girl touches herself and discovers her vagina, even though it feels good, she may recoil.

"It's so scarey," says one youngster. "It's such a deep place of nothing."

Debbie: "I'm gonna get something more and more and more on me. Now I got two earrings. Now I got six feet...."
Her understanding teacher: "Loads of little girls want extra things."

Even though she gets good feelings in the vagina, she may feel the "lack" she discovers as a wound to her pride. She may fantasy that she has "gotten a deep hurt" physically and that she "must sew it up"—at least in her mind. Then, many a little girl begins to deny that she has such a place in her body.

Beatrice had done just this. Although she was now grown-up and had two children and knew (intellectually) that she had a

132

vagina, she kept feeling that as far as sensation was concerned it was still a "nothing." She needed special stimulation of the clitoris in order to achieve any orgasm. "And oftener than not that doesn't work. It's such an insignificant organ. I keep feeling if I only had more. . . . Well, it's so simple for a man. . . ." Unconsciously Beatrice felt that she had lost the bodily apparatus which, as she grew, she gradually came to connect with the ability to gain sexual release.

Strange as it may seem, both boys and girls grow up not only with such old fear-fantasies still in them but fearing also that further injury may come during intercourse so that impotence or frigidity results.

Because of the fear-fantasies that the girl's "bareness" induces inside them, some little boys also build resentments against the sex who brought them such unwelcome ideas.

We used to think that having a chance to examine other bodies minutely might bring real facts to settle the fears. But again this does not touch the fantasies. It may make them worse.

Children need to know that male and female bodies are differently created. Knowing this can be a very comforting fact. Eventually learning the functions of the different parts can also help.

But if the wishes, resentments, fears, and worries are left to fester inside they may form a barrier against a really staunch emotional acceptance of the truth.

Simply telling a child that boys and girls are different takes the physical differences into account. But it leaves the feelings and fantasies untouched.

A child needs to feel that regardless of his sex, he as an individual has deep value to his parents. This is his greatest confirmation. But, in addition, it helps, as always, if we can give children a hand in opening the door to getting their thoughts out in the open where fantasy can be laid beside fact to be compared. And still more important, we need to remember: The

133

facts we offer will prove far more acceptable and will really mean more after the child's wishes, fears, and resentments have been heard. Reassurance that there has been no injury will then carry a more convincing message.

"Holes" Don't Spoil the Whole

To cite an example, in a nursery school Greta is painting a picture, the pattern of which she has repeated time after time: A figure with "ears sticking out like noses"; another with fingers as long as "telephone poles"; another with a nose like a "snake." And "a house with five tall chimneys. No, ten!"

Then all at once Greta is off to the toilet. She stares at Jimmy urinating next to her and her hand moves to where her own anatomy is different. The corners of her mouth turn down and she scowls.

Mrs. Cress, the teacher, realizing that children talk in what they do as well as in words, opens the question revealed in looks and gesture.

"Yes, Jimmy is different, isn't he?"

"I could stand up too," says Greta with defiance.

"I know you'd like to stand up, Greta" (recognizing the wish). "Most little girls would."

Greta's face is shyly grateful. With the door once opened, she shows her eagerness to share what has apparently been bothering her mightily. "But," she says, "they cut off my boy-thing so I can't stand up any more."

"You think they did, dear. Even though they didn't really, it seems that way sometimes, doesn't it?"

Greta nods. "I'd like it back on."

Mrs. Cress nods also. "So it would stick out like ears that look like noses" (repeating what Greta had said of her painting), "so it would stick out like a. . . ."

"Snake!" says Greta, starting to smile.

"Yes, I know, dear, you wish that a lot!"

"Because they always like boys the best." And Greta mutters about how her mother and father prefer her older brother.

"And that makes you angry."

"Uhuh!" with conviction.

"And you wish you'd have a penis like his! And like Jimmy's" (again repeating what she had seen and tying it in with what mattered far more—her feelings about home).

"Then," said Greta, "they'd like me the same." And suddenly, "But, Mrs. Cress, you like girls too?"

"Yes, I do. And I know that they don't need any boy-things. They never really have any. They're whole without."

"They got holes but they're whole! They're holey but whole!" chants Greta. And as she runs off, she sings to the wind, "I'm a girl now."

Had Mrs. Cress closed the door by marshaling scientific facts before Greta's feelings and fantasies had come out, she could never have brought reassurance to her on so firm a base.

Girls are made one way. Boys are made another.

Mothers and fathers look different because they're older, and when children get older they will look that way too.

Diagrams and pictures help visualize realities as children grow, but it helps even more if feelings and imaginings can come first.

(See how Tommy's mother told Tommy about it in the stories that you can use to guide you, too, if you wish, in Part Four. And notice, as you read, how Tommy's mother made room for Tommy to come in with his feelings and fantasies—with his wishes, resentments, and fears.)

You may prefer to use your own words. The general gist is: "Boys have a penis; girls don't. And sometimes both boys and girls think all kinds of things about this" (waiting for the child to bring out his thoughts). "They may think some scarey thoughts, too" (waiting again). "And that makes them mad."

... "They sometimes think maybe something happened. ...
But nothing ever really did. That's the way boys' and girls'
bodies are made."

"A boy has two openings down there," or "two holes." (Children usually call them "holes." Even though a hole can be interpreted as a tear, or as something lacking, the word "hole" seems easier to get than "opening," perhaps because it does help to bring the fantasy out.) "And each hole has its own purpose for

Mother: "What you got in there?"
Daughter: "Oh, just your stockings. I'm practicing for when I grow up."

being," or "each has its own special work." "One hole—the one in front at the end of the boy's penis, its job is for the 'tinkle' or 'weewee' or 'urine' to come out of. And the other one of the boy's two holes—the one in back—that's for the b.m. to come out.

"And girls have three openings or holes down there. The extra one is where the baby comes out. The b.m. hole and the baby hole are *not* the same." (But turn to Story II on page 230 and you'll see how it goes.)

136

11 | Marriage Dreams Begin in Childhood

There comes a time in the life of every little boy and girl when he, or she, falls desperately in love; not with a like-aged person but with a "so-much-bigger sweetheart." There comes a time—too often and too soon denied or forgotten—when every little boy wants to marry his mother and when her father is the prince of dreams for every little girl.

On First Falling in Love

This first time of falling in love with a person of the opposite sex is a crucial and important time in one's sex education. A time of hoping against hopelessness. Of being caught and swung in the shimmering of spider-webbed dreams. Glistening and eery, enticing and frightening all in one.

The feelings which now enmesh one are not little feelings but feelings almost too big for small bodies to bear.

"What nonsense," says one mother, pursing lips and closing ears.

"Let me hear more," says another, who has observed some of the signs in her own youngster. "Just yesterday our four-year-old Patsy really shook us. She put on my best nightgown and ran to her father with outstretched arms. 'Kiss me. Kiss me, Daddy darling. Kiss me like if I was your wife.'"

Some time between three and five, ordinarily, such wishes

137

start. Some children express them openly. Some children more shyly secrete them within their hearts. Some children weave them into their play.

Pat, who is five, is staging a scene of his own making in his older sister's doll house. He puts the father and mother to sleep side by side in their room. He puts the boy doll to bed in the room next door. "It's all dark," he says. Then, humming "Silent Night," he makes the boy tiptoe into the parents' room, takes the mother out of the father's bed and transfers her into his own. At this point, Pat's tune changes to "Here Comes the Bride." Then he has the father doll get up from his bed and leave the house. And with this he hums in merry triumph "Jingle Bells."

Pat's father, who has been curiously watching, wonders aloud: "Did you know what tunes you were singing?"

"Oh yes," answers Pat with a grin. "They're what the boy wants. He wants Mother to be the bride. And Father to be Santa Claus who gives the mother to the boy for Christmas and then goes out to his reindeers and leaves."

Plotting Against One's Big Rival

In Pat's play, the story has moved smoothly. In contrast, Rick, seven, stages a puppet play far more violent. His own running commentary shows its plot.

"The woman calls, 'Help! Help! The father's dragon's after me!' She runs and runs very fast.

"Then her little boy comes and he says to the dragon, 'Down, Dragon. Down. You cannot hurt my wife—I mean my mother.' So the dragon turns and goes after the boy. But the boy fights very hard and beats the dragon. There! The father's dragon's dead. And the father is very mad. 'You've killed my dragon,' he says to the boy. 'I'll kill you!'

"The boy runs to his plane. The father runs to his. Punnhh. Kshreeooummm. Brrrummmm. . . . They fight. The little plane's a jet. It shoots the father's plane down and kshrrr . . . it kills the father. . . .

"And now it's a long time later. The boy has grown up. Here he is with his mother. They love and smooch and do everything a man and wife do.

"And one day the boy said, 'Please, Mother dear, can we have a baby? Please!'

" 'Okay,' said the mother. 'Since your father died I've taken you as my husband and we will.'

"So when Saturday night time came that was their night to make babies and the mother asked, 'Do you want to start our baby now?' So they did. And after sixteen months or so the baby came. It was very late because the boy wasn't sure he hadn't made a mistake to want such a nuisance who might try to kill *his* father's dragon later on."

Most children are not as outspoken as Rick. They may express the wish to marry the parent of the opposite sex but they hold in the rivalry feelings which Rick depicted in the fight between the boy and his father. And they shut in even more tightly those parts that have to do with sex. Perhaps they sense that we might be too shocked if they betrayed to us what one parent described as the "preposterous ferocity and precocity of their thoughts."

"Unbelievable" Wishes Need Believing

Probably no phase of sex education calls for so much courage and so much tenderness from parents as does this time in the life of a child.

The child is now at the age where, if he has progressed normally, the focus of his pleasurable body-feelings has recently shifted to the genital area. His emotional assurance concerning the "rightness" of this shift is still in precarious balance.

Because of this new focus, the child is naturally interested in the role this area plays. He knows that mother and father go

139

to bed together. He knows, too, from his own experiences that body closeness feels good. It's natural and healthy for him, then, to take for granted that love and these good feelings in this special place go hand in hand. But what is puzzling and frightening for him is trying to fit all of this in with the new shape his love has taken for the parent of the opposite sex.

It's hard for parents to think even that the focus of body pleasure had moved during childhood to where it should be when the child grows up. It's hard also to admit that the attachments of the child to parents at this period are as intensely emotional as they are.

Our understanding, however, is vital. Any struggle we ourselves go through to achieve it is worth while. For it is in the successful living through of this period that a child attains not only his basic sense that sexual feelings toward the opposite sex are normal and natural, but a strengthened conviction that sexual acts must be steered and controlled. It is in the successful living through of this period that the child begins to acquire a sturdy sense of sexual morality and the knowledge that sex entails loyalties, responsibilities, reliable devotion. That sex should not become a matter of acting out every impulsive wish.

There are things we can do and things we need to avoid doing in order to help our child move through this important but difficult time. To do them, we must be willing to see and believe that sex has come to rest in bodily focus where it should remain. Our child needs us to assure him of this. He needs us to understand also about his rivalry struggles. He needs firmness from us in handling them so that he may gain firmness of his own. He needs us, moreover, to help him straighten out his confusions and to navigate safely through the great fears that come now and that may too hurtfully stop him from moving ahead.

Fears of Counterattack and Loss

Rick's story gives the pattern: The child's wish to win and wed the parent of the opposite sex, to be married and to have children with this parent. The fantasy, therefore, of eliminating the parent of the same sex. . . . And the little boy's typical desire to destroy the source of his father's strength—his dragon. "The big monster part of him," to use another child's phrase. His penis. His manhood. To the child the envied symbol of his power. . . .

Mother: "Don't worry, darling. Daddy won't be gone long."
Sonny Boy: "I wasn't worried. I was hoping."

But then fear strikes swiftly. "If I knock his off, he'll knock mine and he's so much bigger. I'll run. But he's got legs so much longer, he'll catch up. I'll jump over the cliff into the water. . . ." Letting imaginings loose, "I'll turn into a shark. But he'll turn into a sharker! What'll I do? I know! I'll turn into a little squid. A little iddy biddy squidgey squid, so icky and sticky he'd just laugh and say, 'Oh, that little baby, he's not worth fighting with. Here, Mother! You'd better come and take care of him.' "

In his story he has turned back, as it were, on emotional maturing. If he becomes a very harmless little squid, his father will not recognize him as the rival he would like to be.

A husky six-footer, having trouble in his marriage, doesn't sound too different. "When I start in I finish up so quickly just as if somebody were after me and I had to get through fast. I'd rather touch my wife's breasts. I'm no man really. Not in bed. Not anywhere. . . ." It's as if he too were thinking, "If I stay a baby, the person who's after me for having this woman will look on me as a helpless little thing and not as a rival who must be fought."

The little girl's wish to outrival her mother is no less intense than is the little boy's to outrival his father. But we do not ordinarily realize the strength and tenacity of such wishes.

Nonetheless it gradually dawns on these children that they cannot wholly possess the person whom they love the best. They then imagine painfully that they are being rejected. And anger rises against the best beloved as well as against the rival.

> They are angry at *the parent of the same sex* for being *in their way*. They are angry at *the parent of the opposite sex* for *not giving them their way*.

In their minds they have neither parent to rely on. It is hard to find their own path through the maze. They become frightened and confused.

Ruby, for instance, says, "These days it's so confusing. I hate them both so much, I could burn them. Only I'd be an orphan then and I'd hate that much more."

Even when feelings are less violent, children still become afraid both of what they imagine they might do and of the consequences they fantasy might follow. Something precious might be taken from them. Love certainly. Or some cherished possession.

In a nursery school a little girl grabs a toy engine from a little boy. He stands and shrieks, "She took my penie."

More often such fears come out in disguised ways. Many

children, for instance, fear the doctor and the doctor's "shots" or that the nurse with the hypodermic needle will hurt them far more than is realistic. They fear the dentist. The barber. To many, any approach to the body may be interpreted as having hurtful intent, the danger lies so keenly in their minds. For this reason it is wise, if possible, to avoid tonsillectomies and the like between the ages of three and six or so, during the most intense stretch of this love-rivalry period. This applies to girls as well as boys.

As we saw earlier, whereas the little boy feels "This might happen!" the little girl feels "Even though something has already happened, worse could come." It is all very vague. But, she worries, Mother might take something more from her.

One aspect of this fear has to do with her wish for a part of Father which she feels is Mother's claim.

Jan sings:

"I'm hungry,
I'm hungry
To get a fat tummy
To get a fat baby
A fatso daddo's
Baby beanie
Beanie baby
Right in here!
Then I'll have a piece of my Daddy
For keeps."

This has its happy counterpart later. Unless too great anxiety gathers, its carryover into adult life can contribute to a woman's wish to have babies as a part of the man she loves.

But when one is a little girl, such wishes make one fearful that Mother may come along and reach in somehow and take away what one has no right to have.

Remnants of this side of the picture can also stretch into

143

adulthood. Among these are discomforts during pregnancy, fears of being hurt or cut during childbirth, unease during menstruation (as if the blood were a sign that hurt had been done), and the fear of anything entering into this part of the body, so that intercourse is not the welcomed and welcoming act it should be.

Some Things that Make Fears Grow Worse

Sometimes parents unwittingly make these fears mount. If, for instance, a baby arrives in the family and we encourage a child to feel that "This is *your* baby" instead of "your sister or brother," we can set fantasies moving at a higher speed.

This is as true for a boy as for a girl. As with anything else that seems to give a child permission to take a parent's place, it makes the fantasy of danger more real.

Especially frightening are constant "loverish" contacts. The story of Matt brings a case in point. His father died when Matt was six. After the funeral, his grandfather put a kindly hand on Matt's shoulder. "You're the man now. Remember that, Matt." His grandmother sobbed through her tears, "Be good to your mother. She hasn't got your father anymore." His mother, moreover, in her loneliness turned to him. She took him into her bed at night.

Little Matt wanted to take care of his mother. Little Matt wanted to love her to make up to her for the love she had lost. Little Matt wanted to be what he could not be. He wanted to be his mother's man.

And fear grew in him. And fury too. Fury at himself for his own incapacity. Fury at her for her expectations, for putting him into a false position. The hard wad of fury grew. But Matt did not voice either his wishes or his fury. They went under in him and were lost from his sight.

When Matt married, he found himself feeling that his wife's

144

sexual wants were "too demanding." Even though he saw that they actually weren't, he nevertheless kept getting angry and seemed driven, as it were, by unaccountable fits of roughness which seized him during the sex act.

Inside of himself, big Matt still felt the fear that little Matt had felt when too extreme body closeness had brought good body-feelings focused where they normally would be focused in a boy of his age. Big Matt was still trying angrily to disprove little Matt's fear.

Nonetheless, intercourse became less and less frequent. Matt retreated into business as if satisfaction in his big job might take him back to the time when he had felt safer.

In Matt, as in any child, if anxiety grows too grave, he—and she—may turn back emotionally in growing up. The girl may deny her important love for Father, treat him shabbily or disdainfully, transferring this later onto other men. She may seek to woo Mother in order to make peace with her in this manner.

The boy in his need to hide the part of himself which he feels most in danger and at one and the same time to get legitimately close to Mother "like a girl does with a girl," may turn more feminine. He figures also that this may make Father more gentle with him, "the way he is with Sister."

Even though most children are not confronted with the overwhelming temptations that frightened Matt, they may be inadvertently stimulated in lesser ways.

Sybil, five, had during the past year developed many strange little fears. "What, we wonder, are we doing?" her parents asked.

When Sybil was given the opportunity to confide in a therapist, she showed how certain situations had started her imagination traveling in frightening directions. "I wish you'd talk to my Daddy," she said, "about throwing people on the bed. He

145

bounces me back and forth. What a pill! He thinks he's the boss of my bed and my bedroom. He dashes me this way and that way. What a man! Only it's very dangerous. You know, it might hurt your fanny. I hate that Daddy! That's no way to treat a child."

The boy, too, when roughhoused, enjoys it but may imagine also that he will be hurt. And yet, roughhousing, jouncing, and tickling are things we may do without thinking. Kissing our children on the lips, letting them see us continuously when we are not clothed, letting them come into our beds or going into theirs, lying down with them—these are all better avoided. (We can see even more clearly now the need for parental privacy mentioned in the last chapter.) Wishes are stimulated and so are anxieties.

When a child comes in on occasion seeking refuge from a frightening nightmare, we do best to take him back to his own bed and to sit by his side for a while in a comforting nearness. This may prevent the occasional nightmare from turning into a frequent occurrence which serves as excuse for barging into an intimate situation which the child desires but essentially fears.

"I like to squeeze in the middle between my Daddy and Mommie and shove them apart," Tad grinned. But a moment later he stumbled over a toy and bumped his knee.

"He's forever hurting himself," his father exclaimed.

"So he needs to be comforted," his mother put in. "I'd hate to refuse him the comfort of coming into our bed. It would only make him more unhappy."

This brings us to a curious phenomenon which appears to have come about in our time and our culture. In contrast to the classical picture of the son's fearing the father most during this stage of development, a fair number of little boys today seem to feel that their gravest hurt will come from Mother. Perhaps one reason for this is that the mother has, in fact, become the most dominant person in many homes.

146

Actually some downright and straightforward but kindly refusals make children happier. Talking openly about feelings, too, helps settle the turmoil.

The parents' group which Tad's parents joined discussed these matters.

"I told Tad we'd been making a mistake to let him come into our bed," Tad's father reported. " 'Parents need privacy,' I said.

" 'Okay, then I'll get in on *your* side Daddy,' Tad answered quickly.

"That had me puzzled. But I saw what he meant when he exclaimed to his mother, 'If I talk to Daddy, he won't get around to kissing you.'

"You should have seen his mother then. She literally beamed. 'You really want to come in on *my* side!' she answered. Only she didn't say it as if she were mirroring *his* feelings. She said it as if she were speaking quite clearly for herself." . . . As we've said so often, it's not only what you do that counts, it's how you do it. Your feelings come through.

"Well, anyway, then I decided it was about time for me to be a man. So I said to Tad, 'You sound, dear, as if you'd like to keep Mother from me. Most little boys would. But their daddies won't let them. And their mommies had better not either!' At which my young son looked at me in astonishment. Then he shook his head at his mother, 'You got to listen to Daddy, you hear me? He and me know what's best.' "

Essentially there is a deep wish in every man-child and woman-child psychologically to fulfill biological destiny. The kindly firmness with which Tad's father had spoken brought Tad a firm footing. As if he could now say to himself, "I'm going to get support from my father. I have him to copy in becoming a man."

Quentin, in contrast, complained, "My mother, she says she

and my daddy work like a football team. But if you ask me, she's always the captain. It's she who hikes the ball and rams it into a forty-foot fellow. If she can knock *him* out, what chance does a little guy have? I wish my father wouldn't mousy-foot around."

But when Quentin's father knew how important it was for his son to feel his father's strength to identify with, he did better. "Oh boy," Quentin exclaimed, "you should have seen him. He was good! Yesterday when my mother said, 'You wear *these* clothes!' like she always does, he spoke up and said, 'No.' It used to be he'd wear these clothes. But not yesterday. When he came downstairs he'd politely put *these* clothes back in the closet. He was in his own choice suit." And then with shoulders squared, "When I'm married I'm going to be like he was yesterday, not like he was before."

For the girl, seeing Father at the helm is also important. Deep down inside her every woman wants her man to be strong and gentle. To cherish and lead and protect her.

All of this does not mean, though, that Father should be a cave man and Mother a shrinking violet. It does not mean that Mother should lack definiteness and firmness. Her children need to feel such qualities in her. They need to feel her as strong and sturdy but not as a person who must always "hike the ball."

Just as the boy needs a manly man with whom to identify, so also does the girl need a womanly woman. Children of each sex need healthy contacts with the parent of the same sex to foster and strengthen identification. A little boy's wearing an old tie of his fathers and strutting after him proudly. A little girl's wanting to bake a small cake while her mother bakes a big one. Such acts, for instance, bring evidence of the wish to copy. But this does not mean that the son becomes a duplicate of the father nor the daughter of the mother. To copy does not mean to become a copy. It merely gives the underpinnings upon which to build one's own structure.

The child takes into himself, as it were, his parents' strengths, their restrictions, their limitations, their ideals. These he makes into his own—his own codes, his own morals.

If they have no tolerance for his love feelings and for his body sensations, he may develop a lack of tolerance for these in himself. If they raise no barriers to his acting out his wishes, he may feel that he can go after whatever he wants in life without restraints.

Again, two things are called for: Parents are needed to listen to a child's wishes with genuine sympathy for the pathos of them, the push and the turmoil. "I know you feel this way." . . . "Every little boy wants to marry his mother." . . . "Every little girl wants to marry her father."

But healthy opposition is a must so far as the acting out is concerned.

Olive's father took both things into account. He soon caught on to what was happening when his five-and-a-half-year-old daughter kept calling for him at night to bring her a glass of water, a piece of apple, to pull the curtain, to give her one more hug.

"Look, darling," he said, "I think you're doing these things to keep me here with you."

"Well," Olive countered, "you're a man and I'm a woman. What do you expect?"

"But," said Father, "I've got Mother. She's my woman. . . ."

"Then you've got two women and I'm just waiting to see which one you'll finally choose. . . ."

"Look, dear," said Father, sitting down quietly, "lots of little girls feel the same way. It's natural to want to call their father away from their mother and to try to be their father's woman. You're my little girl whom I love very much. And Mother's my woman. I've chosen *her*. But I know you don't like that at all."

"No," said Olive. "No, I don't. But some day she'll get old and die. And then you'll have no more choice."

Father smiled, rose, patted his little girl.

"You see, dear, childen can't ever marry their parents. But you're mad at Mother anyway. And at me too for choosing her."

"Uhuh, I am. And I wasn't going to give up, either. But I guess I've got to. You're so stern. . . . Oh well, when I grow up I'll have the same problem with my little girl. I'll have the daddy and she'll be jealous of me."

Olive was fortunate in having a father who knew how to credit the seriousness of her wishes. He could let her come out with her feelings, and still let her know with firmness that the acts which took him away from Mother were not in order.

"Your mother's my woman; you're our little girl" or "Your father's my husband; you're our son." . . . "I know you'd like to get between us in bed . . . come into our bedroom . . . separate us somehow" (whatever you may notice your child doing). . . . "But this is not allowed" or "I know you'd like to be rid of me. But you can't, dear. I'm here to stay. . . ." Both Mother and Father need to say these things.

Incidentally, your child may not have brought such thoughts out directly. But as you become more sensitive to what he is living through, you may get the kind of signs and clues we have talked of. A little girl's calling Daddy constantly away from Mother. A little boy's pushing into the car beside Mother, inching Father aside. . . . Then perhaps you can lead the way to greater frankness. You might say, for instance, "I imagine that sometimes you'd like to be the father [or the mother] around here. Only no child can really take Father's or Mother's place." And be sure to add often enough, "And it naturally makes you angry," so that your child knows you stand ready to help him handle these feelings too. ("You can draw what you'd like to have happen to me or write a story about it, or tell it to me straight out.")

As for the good body-feeling part of the picture—and the most difficult one for us to endure—understanding is especially needed. One finely attuned mother said, "I can see it all so clearly now. That small temptress of ours feeling sexy toward her father in her own painful, puzzled, childish way. Astonished, I imagine, by sensations she desires but is also afraid of. She was masturbating some time back. And I can see the mistake I made. I said something foolishly about keeping her hands away from there. So instead she started again to suck her thumb—going back to a more babyish stage for the comfort that one's body can bring. I can see the why of this too. Even though she can't be the most important person in her father's life, it must hurt her pride not to be. So she needs comfort. I've got to let her know I made a mistake and it's all right for her to get those good body-feelings. . . ." As we said in the last chapter: Some parents are able to take this attitude and to say to their children, "Alone in bed. That's the only way children are allowed to have these good touchings." (This channels the outlet of the feelings and helps build controls.)

Meanwhile wholesome contacts are needed also with the parent of the opposite sex. Both in times alone together and in family times. And it's good, too, to have a child help the parent of his sex do appropriate things for the parent of the opposite sex: "We'll go get a birthday present, Son, for you to give your mother." "And Daddy, please, a heap of valentines so I can send one to her every day."

Children can play out many of their feelings in family play, play with dolls or with animals. "I'm this puppy's father," says Jon. "I'm it's mother," says Jane. "Okay, I'll go down to my work and bring home the meat for him." "Okay, I'll do the cooking and change his diapers."

Obviously it is much simpler to help guide a child through this love-rivalry period if the parents are solidly together. It's easier for everyone if he can know with inner assurance, "Father and Mother love each other. We had you come to us. Our place is with each other and your place is with us."

151

If parents are divorced—actually or emotionally—each may feel more need than he otherwise would to turn to a child for his own completion. Out of one's own loneliness one may desire to hold a child too close.

Should this be the case, we do best to admit it to ourselves, to guard against it as much as we can, and to seek professional help if need be.

When contact with a father is lacking, we can help both boy and girl to establish contact with another man. A man teacher in school, a playground director, a swimming teacher, grandfather, cousin, uncle or, finally, Mother's new husband. The boy's primary aim will be to have a man with whom to identify; the girl's to have a man to "adore." However, trouble may spoil the good that can come of this substitute father–child relationship unless we realize that as intimacy increases the substitute father will fall heir also to the mixed feelings that would have gone to the real father were he still around. In addition, the child may shunt off onto the substitute father the anger he feels at the real father for having gone away.

When Lorene's mother noticed that Lorene was alternately clinging and acting haughty to her uncle, she commented, "You sort of wish Uncle Buzz were Daddy, I think."

"Yes I do," said Lorene.

"And you're angry at him for not being Daddy, and at me, too, sometimes for not having kept your Daddy nearer where you could see him. And mad at him for going away. . . . I get mad at him and at myself, too, for not having been able to work things out and stay together. . . ."

"Not mad at me?"

"No, dear. Children aren't ever really to blame for their parents' leaving each other. Though they feel at times that they are."

Such recognition of feelings and such reassurance can help counteract the self-condemnation that a child senses, especially

152

if a separation comes about during the love-rivalry period. As if his wishes to separate Father and Mother—to possess one and be rid of the other—had been the cause.

Even where parents are getting along well together and where no separation or divorce is contemplated, a child may fear that it will because of the wishes he holds inside.

As for encouraging the child's anticipation of growing up and marrying later, we may bring it in hopefully, "When you grow up, then you will have a husband [or wife] all your own."

Outwardly the child may meet this with protest. "No," says Prudence. "No, I won't get married with anyone my age. If I can't marry my daddy, I won't marry anyone. I don't want to marry any skunky little boy." Inwardly, nevertheless, the foundations of marriage are being built.

We need to be kind. Firm. Tolerant.

We cannot help smiling occasionally. But beneath the smile we need to feel tenderness. No scoffing or disbelief. To our child these feelings are serious. They need to be respected essentially. For out of our respect for his feelings will grow his respect for how he feels eventually toward himself in his relationship with the opposite sex.

12 | More about Bodies, Babies, and Birth

All at once, suddenly—or bit by bit, gradually—children's questions and wonderings rise to the surface. When we are firmly established on an emotional basis of understanding children's attachments and body-feelings, we can turn our attention with greater insight into bringing to children the kind of answers they seek. We can help them get their concepts clear.

Nor will we neglect feelings and fantasies. For if a child's facts of life are to become his to live by, he must separate them from the fictions he imagines. And he does this best as fact and fiction are laid side by side where they can be plainly seen and compared. (You might re-read the section on "Clearing the Way for Sex Information to Take" in Chapter 7, pages 92–97, before going on if this point isn't clear.)

Where Does the Baby Come Out?

Sooner or later after a child has absorbed the fact that a baby grows inside his mother in a special baby-growing room, or uterus, he begins to puzzle about how the baby gets out.

As with many other things, he uses what is familiar to him to explain what is unfamiliar. He may have been told quite factually that the baby comes out along a passageway called the vagina through an opening that lies between the mother's legs.

But his own mind when he is young doesn't leave it at that. He struggles for something he can grasp more clearly, something more on his level. He figures: "The baby comes out down there." He has gotten that much. "I know something else that comes out down there. My b.m.'s do." So, what could be more natural than to imagine that the babies come out of the same opening?

Another common fantasy is that "The mother will burst apart." This harks back to earlier notions of exploding which are current during toilet-training days when the child felt at moments that his own tight little tummy would burst.

These and other fantasies emerge when children feel free to express them. What happened in Mrs. Anderson's kindergarten illustrates this. In the meetings which she held regularly with parents, they had asked for her help. The school principal had added his approval. And so Mrs. Anderson prepared herself to meet what might arise.

Even so, it came unexpectedly one day when the children were discussing something quite different. The class had gathered on the rug to talk about not teasing people. And Millicent said, "They teased my mother 'cause she got so fat. They didn't know she was going to have a baby. But when it came out she got all thinner again."

That started them off. And Mrs. Anderson, knowing the importance of hearing what children have on their minds, listened before she began to explain. "In fact," she said, "I first turned the question back very simply. I asked them what they thought about it; what they'd guess."

As she had anticipated, several thought "The baby comes out of the seater," "out of the b.m. hole."

"But," there were protests, "you can't stretch that much. A baby's bigger than the biggest b.m. . . . If you did, who'd stretch you back so the b.m.'s wouldn't keep falling all over?"

"The baby could burst out of the mother's belly button."

"It would burst a round hole in her."

155

"They'll have to cut her."

"That's what they did to my mother," from Sam. "My mother went to the hospital and lay down on the doctor's bed. And the doctor got a scissors and sterilized it and cut the mommy open. Up to the chin."

There was lots of emphasis on cutting. A good many children brought it in. Mrs. Anderson wondered: "Why?" "And then suddenly," she said, "I began to understand at least one part of it. It was when Benjie put in quite gaily, 'They might've cut my baby brother too. Then he wouldn't have gotten alive to pest me so much.' That made me realize that some of such imaginings were wish-fantasies, as if the child, with one side of himself, wanted, as it were, to have both the mother and the new baby punished. But there were fear-fantasies also mingled with such wishes. 'Mommy might get hurt too much!' and 'When I have a baby I don't want to get cut.' "

So Mrs. Anderson said she knew sometimes children didn't feel so good about their mothers having new babies. Sometimes they wanted, sort of, to have the mommy get hurt to punish her for having it and they wanted something to happen to the baby, but these were worry-making wishes. She could see that the children were worried now. And she wondered if they mightn't like to know two things: First that their wishing couldn't actually make anything happen. And second, that "really, truly the baby has a much better way of getting out."

"Where, oh where?"

"There's a passageway that leads from the baby-growing room to the outside."

"You mean like a hall?"

"You mean like a tunnel? So the baby can go through it and come out of a ready-made door?"

"Yes, out of a passageway with a ready-made door called the vagina. A really stretchy opening, that can stretch much bigger

156

than the b.m. hole and then stretch back, like this elastic band does. See? It pulls wide. And then . . . ?"

"It unstretches."

"It goes again to how small it was."

Reiteration of the fact that there are three openings in the girl in contrast to two in a boy comes in very helpfully at this point, as does also a repeat of their functions. (See page 136, and Story II in Part Four.)

To help you tie it all together in relation to the birth process, turn also to Story III on pages 233–235.

Around seven or eight, and from there on, children will want to know how the baby grows inside the mother. (See Story IV.) They will be interested then also in seeing straightforward and clear pictures of birth. (You will find pictures of this sort in Story V.)

How Do Babies Start?

Probably the hardest question of all to answer is the one that inevitably enters a child's mind, whether he asks it or not: "How does the baby start?"

Before tackling this in terms of answering our children, we need to look for a while inside ourselves: Why is this question so difficult? Why is it so embarrassing?

Parents have voiced it: "Because we somehow don't want our children to know that we enter into this kind of union. We have come to it in our own lives with our own kinds of hesitations, with our own great or small anxieties. Isn't it too much for children to know about the great and wonderful surgings that the sex act should rightfully bring? How can we tell them about intercourse without betraying the fact of our own passion and ecstacy? Or our wish to obtain this, if we do not? Our intimacy? Our joy in each other? Our fulfillment of love?

Curiously, children sense our feelings. Children detect it if

157

we obscure the fact that pleasure is or should be had as two bodies come together. They sense, too, from where "those curling currents spread." The source. The place in the body that generates the "sparkings" that make you feel "so shivery and blush."

And this is good.

As they grow they need to control acting on this knowledge —yes—and they can do so. But hopefully. With the bright outlook that someday these deep pleasures will be theirs. Not because of fear or guilt.

"We—your parents—have these pleasures. Want these pleasures. And it is your birthright someday to have them too. It's long waiting. Hard waiting at moments. But necessary to wait. Meanwhile you can channel acting on these feelings, as you know already how to do—necessarily, only by yourself. Later, the good feelings which you can give yourself at night will be more fully rounded, more meaningful because they will be a part of loving the person whom you love best in the whole wide world."

We may say none of this, or only small parts of it, aloud. But when we can say it to ourselves something happens inside us that frees us to help our children more.

"However," as one mother admitted, "we usually talk about sexual intercourse to our youngsters as if it had to do only with getting pregnant."

"Perhaps," said a father, "we've made it too scientifically anatomical. Could that be one reason why children these days seem to think nothing of it and go haywire in their teens? Perhaps we are so afraid of betraying that we ourselves have sexual feelings that we try to make it too coldly factual. After all, with most people intercourse is not alone for procreation; it's for intimacy and sexual completion—and we hope it always will be for the expressing of love."

And so, when our children wonder about babies starting, let's not omit the love part of it: the fact that man and woman come together physically for the intimacy and good body-feelings, for the warmth and the sense of completion—not only when they want a baby but when they want to be as close as two people can get.

They meet and they love and they marry. They establish a home. They cherish each other with a mutual sense of responsibility. And out of this union and out of many times of being physically together which furthers the bond between them, grows the wish to bring their baby into the world.

How is it done? The same way as the closest of loving. The husband puts his penis in the wife's body in the special place called the vagina. (The most grown-up way to speak about this is to call it "sexual intercourse".) This is the ultimate fact. But so many things enter in. To see how some of these may be included when you tell it to your children, turn to Story VI in Part Four of this book.

As for a few more biological details about the baby's starting: A part of the baby comes from the father. A part is already waiting in the mother. These two little parts are so very tiny, you can't see them except under a strong microscope. And neither one alone can start to grow into a baby—not till they meet and join.

"Oh, they're like half-seeds," said Jim, while Ginny added, "They need their partner to get to work."

The part from the father is called the sperm cell and the part in the mother is called the egg cell (or "ovum"). And when they join, they flow together and make just one single baby cell (called a "fertilized egg cell" or "fertilized ovum"). (There's more of this for you in Story VII, Part Four.)

Probably your child will wonder too: "Where do the sperm cells come from in the father?" And you can tell him, "From two sperm manufacturing places right under the penis. You've

159

probably called them 'balls.' Their grown-up name is 'testicles.' They begin to manufacture grown-up sperm cells when a boy starts to become a man and they continue to all through life by the millions.

"And where does the mother keep her egg cells? She has two little storage places called the 'ovaries' up inside her, one on each side of the uterus or baby-growing room."

If you happen to have had a Caesarian, you can say, "Once in a very, very, very great while a mother's opening can't stretch enough to let the baby through. So the doctor has to put the mother to sleep and then very carefully cut an opening through her tummy to let the baby out. And then he sews it all back together again." And be sure here again not to forget feelings. "It sounds pretty scarey, but that is not the usual way a baby is born."

Should your child be adopted, you can tell him that although you wanted a baby to grow inside you, it just didn't happen. Therefore he had another seed-daddy and another seed-mother (or "biological" father and mother) and that he was started and was born the same way as any other baby. And then, because his biological father and mother could not keep him, you adopted him and he became yours. And—the feelings again— "Sometimes, I imagine, when you think of it, it makes you angry that you didn't come from our seeds. So are we. But in our love feelings you're just as much ours. You belong in our family." And then, because the adopted child may be needlessly fearful that we may abandon him as his biological parents did, especially in moments when his feelings toward us are not positive, we can add on occasion: "Even when you feel you don't like us, you still do belong."

As the child grows older, he will—around ten or eleven probably—want still further facts: For one thing he may want to trace the path that the sperm cell takes when it goes from the father's penis up into the mother's vagina and higher to join the egg cell or ovum. He will be interested to learn that the sperm and egg, now joined into one fertilized cell, fastens itself onto the inner wall of the uterus, where it will develop into a baby. (For these facts, turn to the pictures and descriptions in section VIII in Part Four.)

We said much earlier: Children get their information and build their concepts through seeing, hearing, "catching attitudes" as it were, and bringing to bear on their impressions many of the curious and primitive fantasies which they have kept inside from an early age.

By the time a child asks, or is interested in the father's part in procreation—usually somewhere between five and eight, though it may be sooner—he has begun to be aware of man–woman relationships. And so, what we have been saying about including the emotional side of the picture fits in with his developmental concerns.

But natural to the child's development also are feelings and fantasies that may counteract his accepting the positive, loving aspects we have stressed. He not only feels, but he envies—as we saw in the last chapter—the intimacy of his mother's and father's "being snug together all of every night." He is too old to snuggle with the good baby pleasures that are a dim part of his past, but a profound part nonetheless. He is too young for mature closeness. He is lonely and jealous at times. Angry at father, angry at mother, angry at the whole business of their being close.

"No, no, no!" protested a seven-year-old when she was given the facts of how babies start. "I won't have my daddy get that close to my mother. I'd rather have the stork." But after she had had many opportunities to voice her anger, she grew easier. And the barrier against accepting the positive part of the picture let down. "Yes," she said now, "in my mind I see Daddy and

161

Mother in bed together. They look so joined together. So good and so cozy and happy. Talking together in the nearest whispers. Someday my husband and I, we'll be that way too."

Seeing in one's mind, however, and actually seeing are two different matters. When a child sleeps in the same room with his parents, he inevitably observes their union. They may believe him asleep. But something of the act reaches him. He does not always stay asleep.

Hubert, a boy of ten, recounts, "When I was six and in my parents' room, I'd pretend to be asleep with my eyes squidged up just a fluttering slit open so my parents wouldn't get suspicious. I wanted to see. But I got oooo!—most terribly scared. My father was like a dog with rabies. And I thought my mother would get killed."

A man, married for several years, has not been able to get over such early impressions. "I wondered," he says, "what kind of business was this? They seemed crazy. They'd do mayhem one or both to the other. It was frightening. But someway tempting too."

As we know, when wishes impossible of fulfillment are too tempting and grow too big, fears and angers grow too big also. And the overgrown feelings interfere with a positive acceptance of sex.

From all of this and from what is known today of human beings and their problems, it is best that children brought up in our type of culture should not sleep in the same room as their parents. Nor—as we mentioned earlier—should the door be left open for them to wander in.

Where living conditions are crowded, this posits a very real dilemma. "We thought it impossible," reported one mother, "but when we saw how important it was, we turned our living room into a studio bedroom and put Hanny in the regular bedroom. It worked out all right."

This brings us to another problem which modern conditions of life impose on us. In many homes and apartments, the walls are none too soundproof and children are bound to hear some of what goes on in their parents' room.

Raymond, five, glowered at his father at the breakfast table one morning. "You're bad. You're bad." He was very apparently both frightened and angry. Finally however, the reason came out. "You bounced my mommy so hard on the bed, you made her cry."

We need to realize that children do often hear things at night and that this is provocative of wish-fantasies and of anger and fear. However, houses are as they are and many people must live in close quarters. Certainly putting up restraints that would hamper normal freedom in sexual intercourse or stopping it "for a child's good" is not good for anyone. Parents do have sex relations. This is part of loving. As we've said, although this is not good for a child to witness, it is good for a child to know. However, we can help him digest it best as we face honestly that in his imagination he may interpret it as frightening and yet be enticed all the same.

This calls for attention to the child's anxiety. It calls for interpretation and for reassurance. We can say simply, "It sounds like a scarey kind of business when you hear those night-sounds in Daddy's and Mother's room. But what really happens is that daddies and mothers get together at night. Very close. And sometimes you'll hear love noises. And sometimes you'll hear love bouncings. You may want to come in. But this is something that parents share together privately by themselves."

Some parents wonder if it benefits a child to see animals mating. The answer is usually "No." Children brought up in the country who are in on the breeding of animals on ranch or farm often carry fear-fantasies with them into adulthood. Importing rabbits or other small animals to illustrate the facts of life does no better. The act is fast. In some animals, rough. And the most essential aspect, that of tenderness, is absent.

Seeing dogs mate, however, often happens by chance. To pull a child away as if the sky were falling or to "beat the dogs apart," as one harassed mother did, fails to relieve the situation. Observing and listening to the child's reactions is, on the other hand, our most helpful step.

A common reaction will be like Annie's, "What are they doing? Making puppies? He's sticking his thinger in her toto." And the next step, "Did Daddy do like that to make me?"

Once again we can fall back on the same principles: "You think the father dog is putting his penis in the mother dog's b.m. place? Lots of children think that's where the babies are started. But it's not. . . ." And you repeat again about the special opening that mothers have. "In a dog it's in the back. In us in the front."

"Oh," very pleased. "That's much better. Then people can hug and kiss."

Some children fantasy that the father "wets into the mother" and that the "baby seeds" are carried in the urine. Many more, as we've seen, imagine that "You get the daddy's penis-seed like you get the mommie's breast-milk. It goes in your mouth and down into your tummy." The fact that the baby comes out below fits in with this notion.

Unconscious remnants of the fact that the very earliest love acts had to do with the mouth when the baby suckled probably have something to do with this too. Then when children transpose their picture of conception and birth to the vagina they sometimes carry along with this transfer some of their earlier imaginings about what a mouth is and does. This mingles with the little girl's fantasies of wanting to have a penis or a part of Daddy to keep. It mingles with little boy's fears of having some-

164

thing happen to his penis: The vagina becomes a dangerous organ. "It's got big teeth in it and hard clamping jaws."

Therefore, at some time or another, when it seems suitable, introducing something very simple about the internal structure of the vagina may be helpful. It can stretch to different sizes. Get big enough for the baby to come through. And be just big enough to fit properly when the penis enters. Some children think it's somewhat like a mouth; and it is in a way, soft like the inside of the cheeks. But it has no hard jaws or teeth in it. It's made to be a comfortable place for the husband's penis to be and for the wife to have it.

How Do Babies Grow When They're Inside the Mother?

Another thing that many children want to know is: "Did I look like me when I started to grow inside my mother?" To begin with the simple answer does best. "At first you didn't look like a baby at all. You were a little tiny round thing, not as big as the head of a pin. And then you looked like a caterpillar, not even as long as your little finger. And finally you got fingers and toes and a nose and . . . (let your child list different parts of himself) . . . and everything else you needed in order to be you."

Later he will be interested to learn that after the sperm cell and egg cell have joined into a single cell, this cell in turn divides into many, many cells. Some of these become bone cells, some will be skin cells, some will be blood cells. . . . Every part of him will develop out of this cell division. And because the original cell came from his mother and father, the baby and the person who grows from the baby will resemble each in certain physical ways.

Small children puzzle also about "How does the baby eat when it's all inside?"

They usually have heard that babies get milk from the moth-

165

er's breast after they are born. So they often conclude that the same is true before the baby comes. They picture a hose running from the source of supply, the mother's breast, straight into the baby's mouth. And when they see pictures of the navel cord, they believe that this is the hose they have imagined. "The baby doesn't eat with its mouth before it's born," we can tell them. "The food comes from the mother straight into the baby's body through a cord or tube that's fastened at one end to the wall of the baby-growing room or uterus and at the other end to the place where your belly button now is." An older child can comprehend that the navel cord (or umbilical cord) takes food and oxygen and blood to the baby and carries away waste products. An older child can also get the fact that there is a kind of thickened spongy tissue where the cord fastens onto the wall of the uterus. This is called the "placenta" or after-birth. It comes out after the baby is born, since it ceases then to be useful.

It is almost impossible to make these things clear to the young child. However, if he asks, "What happens with the baby's b.m.'s?" this fact he can get: "The baby doesn't have to do any till it gets out." And as for breathing? "The baby doesn't have to breathe until it is born." Should he ask, "What do they do with the cord?" the answer is, of course, that the doctor cuts it after the baby is out. "But it has no feeling in it so this does not hurt either the baby or the mother."

"Does the baby move inside the mother? What keeps it from bouncing against the inside of her stomach?" These things are somewhat easier: "The baby grows for nine months inside the mother. And after about four months the baby moves and kicks."

"My goodness," says Sandra, "I saw it kick under your skirt. Doesn't it make your insides black and blue?" "No, it doesn't. Because the baby is floating in a fluid—that is, something like water. And the fluid is a kind of shock absorber. It keeps both the mother and the baby safe from bumps."

166

"Guy!" exclaims Tommy. "When babies are inside their mothers they're smarter than when they get out. They can swim!"

When Brother or Sister Comes

When a new brother or sister is on the way, many of these questions come to a head. Perhaps others also. Some that you possibly won't know how to answer. If so, there's no need for you to worry. You can tell your youngster truthfully that the whole business of having a baby is very complicated and you just do not know everything about it. If he seems to be after something important, you can say you'll ask someone who knows more or that you'll look it up and will tell him when you've found out. Usually what prompts a child to ask a continuous barrage of questions is not so much a wish to know more facts but a wish to have some of his own inner worries relieved: for instance, a wish to know that *he* has your attention in preference to the little stranger who is to arrive.

After all, the coming of another baby is never an unmixed joy. A child feels his mother's conscious or unconscious concentration on the new life within her. He notices, "Her baby-stomach room gets bigger. My sitting lap room gets smaller. It's no fair." He has moments of feeling emotionally as well as physically on the outside, no matter what we do.

We can tell him in advance about the baby's coming. We can let him share in getting the room and the baby's clothes ready. We can tell him that "Mother will be going to the hospital and will be back in a few days." We can see that he gets acquainted beforehand with the person who is going to take care of him if it is to be someone he had not previously known and liked. We can tell him that when the time comes for Mother to go to the hospital, no matter how late the hour, we will come and kiss him goodbye the way we do when we go out for a visit. We can do all of these "right" things. And still he is bound to feel some anxiety. He will feel this especially when Mother is away in the hospital, no matter how well-prepared he has been.

It is well for Father to say, "It doesn't feel good to have Mother away . . . But you can say 'Hello' to her over the telephone" (if this is possible) "and she'll be back very soon." It is well, too, for Mother to send via Father a kiss, a flower, a chocolate, a sucker, as a kind of symbol that she has not de-

Susan: "My goodness, Daddy, that baby's so selfish. No telling how she'll be later on. Even now when she's so little, she takes all of mother's time."

serted her child. Nevertheless, resentment will invariably enter. "I like to be the onliest and the babiest," Judy protested, "and now I won't be none."

This does not mean that a child is "selfish." It means that in some sensitive fashion he recognizes the realignments and shifts that take place in a family as each new life appears.

"Mummy will have to divide her bagful of kisses," remarks young Wally with serious concern.

168

Like Wally's mother, we do well to stress before and after the new baby's birth that "Love is a stretchable thing. When there are two children, the bag of kisses grows twice as big. When there are three children, it grows even more. There's love enough always to go around."

But so far as the bagful of love inside the child is concerned, it will be far more open to receive our love if some of the resentment that collects there can be emptied out from time to time.

More often than not, the child won't open it by himself. He may be too anxious or too ashamed. Such feelings, however, if left inside, may increase his apprehension not only about the baby's birth and about his own sex life later but also about the birth's hurting his mother.

Edith, for instance, kept asking, "Will it hurt you?"

"Yes," said her mother factually. "But the doctor makes the pain less."

"Did I hurt you when I came?"

"Yes, dear. But I got over it quickly. As soon as you were born, I was so glad to have you."

"Will it hurt when the new baby comes?" with repeated persistence. Until one day Edith added, "I hope it does . . . Oh no!" she stammered. "Oh no! I meant, I hope it doesn't." Her slip of the tongue, however, had betrayed what lay underneath.

We do a lot to help our children keep healthy attitudes toward having babies if we can say beforehand and again repeatedly after the baby is born, "Sometimes you'll think that little baby's cute, the way it kicks and wriggles and blinks and yawns. . . . But sometimes you'll think it's a nuisance because it takes so much of Mother's time. And you'll be angry at Mother, probably, when you want her to be with you and she's feeding or dressing the baby. And angry at Daddy too for attention he pays to him or her. . . ."

"And I'll bop you all," David announced.

"No, dear. You'll want to. But that's something we won't let you do." (Differentiating, as usual, between feelings and acts.)

"You may not hit or kick, or do anything like that to Mother or Father or Baby. But," if the child is small, "you may have mother, father, and baby dolls instead to hit or kick or treat as you wish."

"But they're not the real ones."

"I know they're not. And you'd rather do what you want to the real ones. But you can't. You can do it only to the doll ones.

"Or," if he's old enough to talk out his feelings, "you can come and tell us as much as you want about all the mean things you'd like to do but can't really. . . . It's natural to have two kinds of feelings. Kind ones and mean ones. Everyone has."

When the new baby is of the opposite sex, we'll need to remember that children are concerned over bodily differences and that they invariably notice these. If they say nothing of their own accord, we can often forestall worries growing out of proportion by bringing up the matter quietly. "Sister [or brother] does look different. . . ." Then pause to give your child a chance to pick it up; continuing, however, if he or she doesn't. To your son, "I guess sister looks to you as if she had something missing? Lots of boys think that. It's kind of scarey." To your daughter: "Brother has something extra on him that many little girls wish they had, too—sometimes they even think they had them once upon a time. And that makes them sort of scared—but they never really did!" (Go back over Chapter 10 and re-read Story II, Part Four, for more details.)

"But isn't this putting ideas into a child's mind?" one parent asked. "Isn't it better to wait till he brings it up himself?"

Children, however, are least apt to talk about the very things they are most anxious about. Unless we help open the door—

**Children TALK LEAST
about WHAT they
FEAR MOST.
Bringing it *into speech* helps
to take it *out of mind's worries.***

In addition, we need to know that when a girl sees her little brother, she is apt to feel: "He's got more; so you'll love him more too!"

Boys and girls both sense that there is a different quality in the love we give to children of different sexes as well as to different individuals. It's good, therefore, to say quite openly that you love each child differently. And each one a lot.

When an older child sleeps in the same room with the new baby his fears may increase. If he wakes frequently, has bad dreams, wanders about at night, we can surmise that this is the case. He may be feeling that when he falls asleep and loses conscious controls and perhaps dreams about what he would like to do to the baby, he is too close to carrying out his fantasies. Wheeling the baby's crib into the parents' room until they go to bed and then into the living room for a few weeks may relieve the tension, especially if during these weeks the older child is helped to meet his feelings frankly and to get them out in nonhurtful ways.

Another thing to expect is that the older child will want at times to *be* the younger baby. He probably won't say so in words but rather in acts—by talking like a baby, wetting like a baby, wanting more and more of this and that.

Brief periods of playing baby may help tide him over. But good times at his own level should also be planned, with stress on "special privileges" befitting his age. A bit later bedtime, for instance, "because you're bigger now." An extra chance to drive somewhere more often with Father alone. Chances to help plan the family menus on occasion so that he not only feels big and important but also so that he appropriately gets some of the mouth and feeding satisfactions he often envies the baby for.

Where children are perpetually loving to each other, we do well to suspect that all is not well. We can take it as a sign that negative feelings are being held back. We can also take it as a kind of prediction that this child, when grown up, will need to let out in some manner, perhaps onto his own children; perhaps onto husband or wife.

But what if the time has gone by? Let's remember: It's never too late to open the door.

Said Sheila's mother, "Look, Sheila, I've found out I was making a big mistake in telling you it was horrible to feel mean to Sister. You know what? All older children feel that way to the younger ones sometimes. I imagine you can recall things you would have liked to do to Sister at moments but didn't dare. You still can't. But you can talk about them all you want."

When a new baby comes into a family where the other children are a good deal older, their helping with his care can be a fine experience in sex education as preparation for knowing what to do with babies of their own later. But if responsibilities prove too heavy, this can change the anticipation of having babies into a wish not to have any.

Again it's a matter of balance. There are two sides to every coin. Looking at both sides rather than keeping one hidden can in the end make our children more certain of receiving full value in what life brings.

13 | Laying Earlier Ghosts

Whatever sexual matters you discuss with your children you will probably take up again and again. As we've said before, once is never enough. Children need to go over and over what they hear and think. They "get" a part of the picture at one time; another part at another time. In some instances it seems as though they had gotten none of it at all.

Renewing Reviewing

If they do not re-open the subject every so often, if they do not ask any new questions or repeat any old ones, you do well to take the lead. Open it for them so that the communication lines between you are kept open. As you know, your children need the mutual confidence that comes with such sharing.

When there are new puppies or kittens, "They're interesting but not as interesting as humans." When there's a new baby up the block, or a notice in the newspaper of some famous baby's birth, "Remember when we talked about babies being born?" Or during any comfortable time of conversing, "Remember the things you used to think when you were small? And the true things you found out? . . . Remember when we talked about the father's part in having a baby? You don't remember it very well? Okay, let's review it again. These things are interesting. . . ."

If you like, it helps also to mention some of the fantasies

173

which you now know are common. Tell these as you would a folk-tale or story. "Children often imagine thus and so." After all, these are childish folk-tales that most of our children once told themselves. With the retelling, a child may now be able to sever the connections between the facts and fictions he put together in earlier days. But don't pry for old memories. That only does harm.

The years between losing the first tooth and losing the childish shape of one's body form a stretch of time during which children can consolidate many gains in their sex education. It is a time during which earlier confusions can be set straighter. And most important, it is a time in which greater freedom may be found from former anxieties and fears.

The last is particularly important. For when adolesence comes with its push of physical and emotional changing, the more earlier ghosts have been laid, the more securely will a youngster progress.

Shots, Surgery, and Such

In the normal development of every child, certain situations arise which are fear-producing. Ordinarily we try to get our children to face these "bravely." A broken arm or leg. An operation. These we know are frightening. But so are lesser, simpler, more universal things like having a splinter removed, scraping a knee, experiencing a nosebleed, having polio shots, going to the dentist. Even losing the first tooth, strange as this may seem, can ring inner echoes of fears that reach up from the past and make a child anxious about his body and sex. Therefore as part of sex education we need to consider such happenings.

Perhaps the common custom of a child's putting the tooth under his pillow and in its place finding a penny or a present, contains in it some recognition of the event's emotional meanings. One loses a part of one's body. One gets something right

174

away in exchange. As if the wait for the new tooth were too long a time for one's tongue to "feel such a big place of a hole."

Here we are back again at a variation of a familiar principle: It is important in sex education *not to obscure fear by dwelling only on bravery*. It is important to let fear out into the open in order to lay earlier ghosts.

"My tooth came out," says Nicky. Then his eyes grow wide. "Will my toes come out?" with a giggle that sounds a bit hysterical. "Will my toes, my nose, my toto come out too?"

"You're afraid, I think," says Nicky's mother. "Kind of scared that some other part of you might come out like that tooth."

Nicky's hand goes to his penis, clutches at his pants.

Mother puts her arm around his shoulders. Nods. She knows: Lots of children get scared.

Shortly after losing her first tooth, Cindy started having very frightening nightmares. When this persisted, her parents took her to see a psychologist. And here Cindy's fears tumbled out. She thought of her tooth coming loose and from there her thoughts jumped to every sort of calamity. The idea of the tooth and the "raggedy hole" in her mouth, of shots, splinters, the removal of tonsils, of having fallen and cut her leg and its having bled profusely—all of these were jumbled together. Then she remembered having seen some blood in the toilet. It must have come from her mother. "She bled from her vulva. She must have been hurt. Will I bleed too from there?"

Suddenly Cindy's eyes brightened. "Oh dear!" she sighed. "Imagine! My thoughts zigzagged in my imagination from my tooth-hole to my vulva. Isn't that the silliest business?"

A silly business! But, as we've noted before, it happens commonly that imaginings about hurts zigzag from any part of the body to the sex organs.

"You should have seen it when we got our shots in the Army," a man reported. "Some of the men in the waiting line looked positively green. And the men in the line who had just had their shots came out with their hands over their organs, moaning and pretending that's where they got them. It was all a big joke. But even so, some of them actually fainted."

A group of perceptive teachers noted when routine polio shots were being administered in their schools that fear mounted and spread.

"Will my arm come off?" one child asked his teacher.

Another child painted "body pieces" scattered over the paper. "That's what it's like when you get a shot," he explained.

Weeks after, still another child daubed red paint over his hands and face, saying, "Look, I'm still bleeding from my polio shot."

"See!" said a first-grader. "See the dark brown feeling I painted in my stomach? I'm getting a shot and I feel sick in my stomach. I feel just awful."

Along with fear, aggression rose too.

In a sixth grade, the youngsters complained, "That doctor! I never saw such a long needle. Man, he's mean."

Because these teachers knew the importance of letting feelings come out, they said, "Those feelings are natural. So better paint some more and talk some more and act more doctor–shot scenes and share more of how you feel."

Some of the teachers opened the subject up in advance. "Most children are scared. And mad too. Because when you're scared you're bound to be mad."

A first-grade girl did a drawing in chalk. "The doctor is coming to put me up on the table. But I have a pin in my pocket and I'm going to prick him first."

"I'd like to drop him in the Atlantic with his hands and feet tied," from a fourth-grader. And a sixth-grader drew a cartoon of a devil labeled *Me* and a chicken labeled *Doctor,* with the devil saying to the doctor, "So, you're chicken, eh?"

176

Later these teachers reported, "When we were able to carry out such procedures beforehand, we observed that our children were more relaxed, more orderly, and caused less post-shot disturbances than the children who hadn't had a chance to express their feelings." The visiting doctor and nurse in one school were so impressed that they sent for the teacher and asked her how she had prepared her class for the shots.

"Even those of us who did nothing at the time found it was not too late to do something afterward. 'Remember,' we said, 'when you had your polio shots? Perhaps you were more frightened than you let on—and madder too. And perhaps you had feelings about the doctor or nurse—or about your parents for wanting you to have the shots.' "

Again fears and angers came pouring straightforwardly and with honesty, to adults who were fortunately strong enough to accept them and wise enough to say, "This way of letting out is sanctioned; that way is not. No running out of line. One can act courageously even though one feels afraid. There are times and places for telling about and showing one's feelings, as we do in here. But not in the doctor's line."

And then these teachers noticed something of very great importance in sex education. "*After* the children's feelings had come out," they said, "we found that reassurance worked much better than it did when we brought it in before the children had had opportunities to share their fears and their anger." They therefore adopted the procedure of opening the subject by telling needed facts briefly, then attending to the fear and anger, then going back to a fuller development of the facts.

They found, too, that reassurance worked best when it emphasized three points (as it always should in sex education when the body's wholeness seems threatened).

First: The hurt is a passing hurt, it is now all over.

Second: The hurt has left no permanent ill effects (whenever this is true).

and Third: The hurt didn't spread. ("You were hurt only there in your arm. No other part of you was affected, or ever could be.")

In general, after these steps have been taken, children are readier to appreciate whatever valuable outcomes result from the "ordeal." "The shot can save your body from illness and keep you more healthy." . . . "A splinter removed prevents infection." . . . "A tooth's coming out makes space for a new tooth. It's a sign of growing up."

Where surgery is necessary, giving opportunities to get out imagined fears and angry feelings and bringing in reassurances both before and after the operation are measures well taken. (Most of us know that when we ourselves have had to face surgery, even as adults, fear may have led us to imagine all sorts of painful things that never befell.)

The child needs to be told about the coming event frankly and quietly but seriously. The truth that there will be some pain and some bleeding are better not hidden. "It will hurt a little and there will probably be a little bleeding. These will soon be over and you'll be all well again. But meanwhile it will be sort of scarey and you'll be mad at the doctor and mad at us too. Even though you know we can't really help it, you'll probably think we're means as mean can be to let this happen. And you'll be mad at us too for taking you to the hospital. . . ." You'll give your child plenty of chances to tell of his "mads." But if he doesn't, you'll know at least that he has gained comfort from your understanding.

It is important to reiterate both before and after the operation that what is done will affect only one part of the body and no more. "The doctor will take out *only* your tonsils," for instance. "Nothing else. When you wake up, you'll look at your hands and all your fingers will still be there; and you'll look at your face and your eyes and your nose will all be there," and so on. "Only those tonsils that made you sick, they will be gone."

178

It is helpful, too, if you can add enough to be comforting, "Some children are afraid that something may happen to the most precious parts of their bodies which they'll need for loving and having babies when they grow older and where they get their best feelings. But nothing is going to happen to those."

Sometimes surgery is imagined by a child to be punishment due for past "badness," especially for wishes, angers, and body-feelings tied with sexual-emotional development. The wish, for instance, to be rid of the parent of the opposite sex. Or the more ancient wish to smear or to gobble up a parent at whom the child was unreasonably upset.

Separation from the parents when the child reaches the hospital—especially if this is sudden or unexpected—may seem like a confirmation of such fears.

It's best, therefore, if hospital rules permit, to arrange with the doctor to be with the child until he leaves for the operating room, to be on hand so he can see you right away when he comes out from under the anesthetic, and to reassure him beforehand that you will be there when he opens his eyes.

There is one kind of operation that many boys wonder about. They notice the difference in the penises of circumcised and uncircumcised boys. "What made this?" they may ask. "My end sticks out and Drew's doesn't. He's got like a little skin cap. What happened to mine?" asks ten-year-old Charles.

"Differences like that make a boy worry," said his father (turning attention to feelings before facts).

"Yes, Dad, they do. I've noticed that other kids have them like mine but still I think sometimes something must have happened to me."

Father nods. "When you were born, you did have what you say looks like a skin cap over the end of your penis. The scientific name for it is the 'prepuce.' Most people call it the foreskin. And with many babies, when they're still in the hospital after they're born, the doctor removes the extra skin that forms the skin cap. One reason for this is that it's easier to keep the penis clean if its tip is in the open and doesn't have to be slid from under the skin cap to be washed."

"How does the doctor do it?"

"How would you imagine?"

"He cuts it, I guess."

"That's right. He can pull the extra skin over the end of the penis like you can pull your cuff over your hand. And he snips it carefully so it doesn't injure the penis anymore than cutting your cuff would injure your hand. Though the very idea, I know, makes you scared."

"Not as scared now as I was."

The Matter of Sex Play

As we've seen, masturbation is one thing that a child imagines will make punishment descend. Sex play is another. And yet, at one and the same time a child may use sex play in an attempt to counteract fear.

"When I did it alone," one bothered child told the psychologist, "it made me feel all nervous. My grandma'd said it was so wrong. But when I did it with Rollie it made me feel some better. I could think it wasn't my fault. He was egging me on."

Sometimes children enter into sex play to see if others have what they lack or fear losing. They want to compare themselves with others to make sure they're "all right." Some girls, in fact, expose themselves, hoping pathetically to prove that they "have everything." It's as if they were vainly trying to get someone to tell them that their bodies were more perfect than they feel they are. Some boys, feeling that they are so much smaller than Father, want at least to find themselves bigger than some other male.

Many children do have sex play with friends or with sisters and brothers at some time during their lives (usually between four and ten). "We have look games, rolling around games, spank games, tickling and tease games," a nine-year-old confides. Hospital games and doctor games are common among younger children. They offer an excuse for exposure. "The doctor always has you take your pants off and examines you there."

For a variety of reasons, children are curious and eager for companionship in their sexual explorations. By and large, *what they are after in sex play is to get support and sanction for sex feelings or body differences they are not quite comfortable about.*

As they come to accept their bodies, their good body-feelings, their sex, and themselves without a sense of "badness" or inferiority, the need for sex play goes. Many things we have talked about throughout this book have bearing on the matter. Nevertheless, the parent who discovers that his child is having sex play wants to know how to handle the immediate situation.

Punishments, especially physical ones, are least of all to be desired. Hostility to the punisher and increased need for sanction of guilty feelings result and make matters worse.

And yet, the sex play needs to stop. It is not acceptable in our culture. Psychologically if it continues over a long time with physical manifestations, it augments fear and guilt.

Children need their parents' firmness. They need their parents' help to steer them away from continued physical acting out. Parents need to say "No" very definitely. "Such things are not allowed," with kindly but direct authority ruling. "All children have sex feelings. They're good feelings. But children may not experiment with other children to get them."

Discouraging twosomes in the bathroom. Discouraging secret play in closets or playhouse or tents. Encouraging varied activities with friends out in the open. These things are good things to stress when a parent has found sex play going on. It is wise, too, not to have children share the same bed. The body-closeness they obtain is often like an invitation

181

to further stimulation. Where possible, separate bedrooms are advisable. But, most important, as we have emphasized, is to keep clear distinction between feelings and acts.

To give an example: Helen's mother (like Mary's mother whom you read about in the first chapter) came across Helen one day watching with fascination as a neighbor boy urinated behind the bushes.

"My face must have been red," she admitted, "and I did snap at Helen. 'What are you doing?' Anyway, she followed me into the house like a meek little puppy, her face all crinkled with tears. And suddenly I knew how she felt.

" 'Oh, darling!' I said. 'I know I jumped on you. But, Helen, those things aren't permitted' (forbidding the acts); 'they just are not done. But' (turning focus onto feelings) 'they are interesting, I know, and most every girl does want to look. . . .'

" 'I do, I do, Mother,' Helen burst out. 'It's been no fair. You get to see Daddy and I have no boy to look at. And they've got such interesting ornaments on their fronts.'

" 'That you'd like to see, I know. But mayn't.

" 'At least,' said Helen, with a smile dawning, 'at least not till I'm grown up.' "

Later there was more talk and a repeat on bodies and bodily functions. But Helen's mother knew that it was first in importance for her to acknowledge Helen's feelings—to let her child know that her wish was natural but that her actions still had to be steered into acceptable channels.

Sometimes the sex play consists merely of a lot of "talky-talk like 'Hello Mrs. Fanny. Hello Mrs. Tinkle!' " with a scattering of four-letter words appearing out of nowhere.

If we notice a run of such talk done in whispers or with volleys of giggling, and can hold our peace, all the better. Through such means, children of their own accord are managing to channel their feelings into actually nonhurtful acts. If the talk grows blatant, that's something else. (You might like

182

to re-read pages 116–119 at this point.) Again the question arises as to why the child is doing this. Once more we may find that an undue amount of hostility is rearing its head and that other outlets are needed so that hostility does not have to come out in this fashion.

If any sex play becomes too persistent or extreme, obtaining professional services is a wise thing to do.

It's a hard row for parents to hoe. You hoe too widely and you make fear reign. You cut too narrow a swath and you let license grow. So, for your own sake also, when doubt becomes heavy, the professional handclasp may help you a lot.

About Menstruation

Because of the growth and the changes and the upsurge of sexual stirring which take place in adolescence, many of the ghosts that have not found easy resting are then revived. One of the events that connects especially with earlier fear-fantasies is that of menstruation. Curiously, this affects the boy as well as the girl.

As we know, preparing a girl for "menarche"—that is, for her first menstrual period—is essential in sex education.

Most girls start to menstruate when they are around thirteen years old. Some start as early as eleven, a few at ten, and some do not start till they are fourteen or so. Because of this wide variation in age of menarche, even though your own daughter may not be obviously maturing, it's a good idea to discuss it with her before she encounters it in her earlier maturing friends.

Boys, too, should learn about menstruation early, before the time when the girls whom they know are apt to start. For one thing, chance remarks—or even more acutely, chance physical evidences—can be more hurtful if a boy comes upon them unprepared. For another thing, when he is unprepared, he may be more hurtful in the chance remarks he makes to girls.

Around nine or ten is ordinarily a good time for starting in

183

on the subject. Like Cindy, however, a youngster may at any moment during childhood come across signs of a mother's or an older sister's menstruation. If we know this has happened, then, even though the child is considerably younger, the time has come.

We cannot be sure, however, that the telling of facts will automatically set everything straight. With both boys and girls, no matter how carefully we tell them, fear may enter. The thought of blood naturally connects with the idea of physical injury.

One mother, for instance, reports overhearing her seven-year-old boy explain to his five-year-old sister, "You see, Mother was once a bad little boy and had it cut off. She still bleeds now and then."

As we have seen, children imagine that such punishment can descend for a variety of childish misdeeds and "bad" thoughts. An important new point for us in regard to menstruation is to expect fear to be there and to look at it straightforwardly.

When we simply give facts, as if the whole thing were a matter of unemotional concern, we obscure what needs to be a part of the picture.

We can start something like this: "When a girl grows older, you know how her body changes?"

"Yes," either your boy or your girl will no doubt say. "She'll start to get bosoms." . . . "And she'll get a figure. More like a lady."

Then you can go on and tell about some of the inside changes too.

Actually menstruation is a complex matter. First and foremost it is a signal of growing up. It shows that the tiny egg cells that have been in the girl's body since birth are beginning to ripen or mature. It shows, too, that the uterus is getting ready for the time when she will carry her babies securely within her. When that time comes, each growing baby will start, as she knows, from a fertilized baby-cell that must fasten itself firmly to the inner wall of the uterus. For this reason the lining of the uterus must be kept freshly prepared and ready for the baby-cell to root in, just as a plant roots best in fresh soil.

Every so often, then, an extra supply of blood goes to the uterus to help freshen the lining and help anchor the baby.

But suppose no baby is started. Then neither the new lining nor the extra blood is needed by a baby-cell. The new lining, in consequence, begins to grow old and has to be shed in order that another, fresher lining may start. So, out through the vagina come both the old lining and the blood that isn't needed. But one sees only the blood because the lining flakes off in such tiny bits that they are too small to see without a microscope.

This shedding of the extra blood and the old lining is what we call menstruation.

In other words, what one sees is not blood from a hurt; it is blood from a healthy getting-rid of the uterus wall's old lining so that a fresh one can get under way. "This is not hurt bleeding; it's natural or healthy bleeding," is a good thing to say. A woman has a healthy bleeding period every month. "But," returning to giving your child a chance to come to grips with his feelings, "it's naturally scarey to hear about blood or to see it." In this way again the fears are gotten out into sight where they can be compared with more solid facts.

"I know I'll hate it," Susannah protests with the anger that normally accompanies fear. "I don't see why girls have to have it. Boys are lucky. I wish I were one."

When a girl has had chances to get out such feelings and to become familiar early with the fact that grown-up ladies menstruate and that Mommy (if this is true) does so naturally without hurt or illness, then she will be readier and more eager for this important evidence of growing up.

Not all girls, however, feel emotionally ready. Cramps and nausea, aches and sick feelings may come from hidden unhappiness about turning from child into woman.

Coddling is not the answer. Neither is belittling. However, lending a listening ear occasionally to the various complaints that are apt to tumble forth at this time of life may bring emotional support that works better than pills.

But if a girl continues to have trouble, it is a good idea to check with your doctor.

Only under rare circumstances, and only if the doctor finds it absolutely necessary, should there be actual examination of the sex organs. For the young girl starting out on her way to being a woman, such an examination may add another strand to the idea of punishment for secret thoughts. Furthermore, at this age it may seem an invasion of privacy and a kind of violation of the girl as a person.

When a girl first starts to menstruate, she may be quite irregular. She may skip several months between periods. Most women, in fact, remain somewhat irregular. About a third of their cycles extend past the time they believe them due. This is important to know. Otherwise irregularity may be interpreted to mean that something is wrong. Then worry starts. And the tension itself may cause delay.

Another fact we can add is that a woman does not menstruate during the time she is carrying a baby because during that time the lining of the uterus must remain firm and not be shed. We can tell our youngsters also that her periods will stop altogether later in life. This is called the menopause or, more commonly, "change of life" and takes place ordinarily between forty and fifty, sometimes before, sometimes after. But to these young people this is far off. Of greater importance are the more immediate things.

A girl wants to know that her periods normally last from three to six days. She wants to know, too, about personal hygiene—about wearing pads or "napkins," how to purchase them and how to put them on. She may have heard that tampons, or small rolls of absorbent material, are worn by some of the older girls. She may want to wear them. You may have some doubts about the wisdom of her doing so. It's best to check with your doctor. Opinions vary on this.

Discussing the matter of bathing and of exercising is also in order. The old wives' tale about the inadvisability of showering or bathing is not true. A girl needs to pay especial attention to ordinary cleanliness during her periods. Some girls play tennis or engage in other sports they are accustomed to. Some girls prefer not to do strenuous things. It is usually a matter of psychological choice rather than physical necessity. Here again, checking with your doctor will help determine what is best for your particular girl.

As for the boy's reactions to menstruation, he may seem unfeeling and callous. He may tease his sister or girl friends: "What's the matter? Why don't you go swimming?" Despite the information we give him, he may seem totally ignorant. More often than not, such behavior is more than anything else a mask for anxiety. The idea of blood can confirm his ancient, little-child fear-fantasies that the girl has lost something. Irrationally he may wonder: How about me? Perhaps he asks then if boys have something like menstruation.

There are two parts to answering this. One has to do with the manifestations of growing-up-ness; the other with old left-over fears about blood.

You can say that when boys mature they receive an outward signal too that spells growing up. It is called having "seminal emissions." (In the next chapter you will see how you can go into this more fully.) But as far as any discharge of blood is concerned, a boy does not have this. Even so, he may still go on with his fears.

He needs a kindly approach to getting these into the open.

187

One father said to his son quite simply, "Many boys still worry after they know what it's all about. So, even though I've explained it to you, you still can go on connecting the idea of blood with being hurt."

"It does always seem that way, Dad."

"That's natural. I've read that such feelings are a kind of holdover of what many kids imagine when they're little. . . . Lots of small boys think, for instance, that a girl's got something missing. That it got cut off or something equally untrue. And then when they hear about a girl's bleeding during her period, they forget that it's healthy, natural bleeding. Their old thoughts go, 'Hah! That's proof of what I used to think.' It's foolish but natural. A lot of youngsters do imagine that sort of thing."

"That's nonsense," his son protested. "Well, not such nonsense! I see! Not nonsense at all." And his parents noted that he seemed to feel easier about the whole matter after this open comparing of fiction with fact.

14 | Crossing to Man's and Woman's Estate

Comes a time in life when the ordinary parents of the ordinary child begin to think that something is definitely "wrong" with either themselves or their offspring.

"Bratolescence"

As the child approaches and goes into his teens, the attachments between parents and child are sorely taxed. He—and even more she—becomes a more or less obnoxious creature. Critical. Reluctant. Uncooperative. Rude.

"He used to be messy, yes! But now he's filthy." . . . "She used to have disagreeable moments—yes. But now the agreeable ones are as rare as diamonds." . . . "You never know whether she wants to 'doll up' or look like a freak."

From his side of the fence, youth complains: "Parents don't know anything. They're old Yo-yoes. Out of touch with humanity, that's what they are."

"We don't do anything right," declares one parent. "They manufacture occasions out of the blue to pick us to bits."

"It's a nice day," says Father.

"Beautiful," Mother smiles.

"A nice day!" Daughter sniffs. "Well, really! It rained yesterday. And in the spring the sun does have a habit of coming out after the rain. So you have a nice day. Why rave?"

189

Youth says: "What's wrong with my parents?"

Parents say: "What's wrong with my child?"

But underneath, parents worry: "What's wrong with us?"

"We ask our young son to walk his dog. He doesn't. To pick up the litter in his room. He doesn't. To mow the lawn. And he leaves it looking shaggy as a buffalo's hide."

Little sister: "Don't you want to look pretty anymore?"

"We leave our young daughter to do the dishes and we come in and they're still stacked a mile high."

"We're losing control." This is our great fear at a time when control seems so very important.

These boys and girls are young. And the sound of youth calls up thoughts of delinquents on the loose. Calls up thoughts of upsurging sexuality. Calls up our own apprehension. All that we as parents have done in the past seems on trial.

What will come of it if we lose control over this irrational, irresponsible being? He is growing up now. What kind of a grown-up will he be?

We grow tight. He grows tight. And the meeting ground between us is barricaded by mounting tensions. However, through deepened understanding we can often steer our course better and lead him more securely.

Dark Dreams and Dares

Two major tasks now lie ahead for our youngsters: To emancipate emotionally from us, their parents—to become able eventually to put us in second place so that husband, wife, and children of their own may be cherished in first place. And to reach the point where they can establish a durable, mature relationship with the opposite sex—a relationship in which they may give of themselves and enjoy sex fully without being hampered by unnecessary fears and guilts.

Meanwhile, emotionally speaking, we might call their present time of life a period of *dependent independence*. The independence isn't real. It's a cover-up for dependency that youth is trying to shed.

Our child has reached a turning point. He stands on a bridge that spans that space of being "too old to be a child and too young to be a person," to use one girl's words. Can he take the highroad that leads to true emotional independence? To confidence in the ability to take care of himself and to give himself in lovingness to a family of his own? He knows vividly how inadequate he still is for such tasks.

He feels small at many moments. As uncertain as the uncertain form of the changing body that houses him. Uncertain in unfulfilled male–female relationships whose culmination cannot be sanctioned. Beset by sexual impulses that he too often feels he must not enjoy. Struggling too often not to masturbate, and yet turning to it in spite of himself with extreme guilt and

191

with self-condemnation that cuts down the confidence in himself which he so sorely needs to help him progress.

He goes to school with masses of children, often so many to a teacher that he fails here also to find the identity he is seeking.

He lives in a society where competition is the keynote and where comparatively few can successfully gain the bigness of being among those in first rank.

And what sustaining promise can he hold for his future? What peaceful security can he anticipate with assurance in this atom-threatened world?

The huge unknown that descends from the outside meets the doubts that rise from the inside. He is pressed in between.

Where can he turn for closeness, to feel at least a wellspring of emotional warmth and support?

The low road beckons. He naturally has moments of yearning for old protections that whisper from his far-distant past. Like an infant, at times he unconsciously longs to crawl back into the curved shelter of his mother's arms.

But giving in to this would spell death to youth and to his new-growing selfhood.

If he were to give in to it, it would mean canceling out the deeper gifts to come later in sexual union. He would have to draw heavy black lines through acquiring the maturity that brings contentment with a home, a family, and children of one's own.

And so he must whistle to gain courage. He must hide unsureness. He must fight it. He unconsciously dredges up every real and imagined cause for anger in his attempt to push away and separate himself from those on whom he wishes so desperately to depend. His parents. His mother most of all.

But his maneuvers do not work. He needs us even though he wants to throw us over. He fights. We fight back. If he fights harder, then we condemn him more and forbid his protest. He feels as valueless as a flyspeck about to be flicked off into nowhere. He feels guilty and afraid. Isolated and angry. Lost and lonely. Thrown back into an uneasy renewed need of us. Chained to us by resentment and the continuing wish to get even for not being able to get away.

And then—

The BONDAGE of GUILT-RIDDEN RESENTMENT RETARDS the adolescent's PROGRESS far more than the BONDS OF LOVE.

Although it's natural for the boy at this age to go with other boys, if he needs to bolster himself unduly he may turn more blindly to them. To an undesirable gang, possibly. Not only for the more normal reason of feeling self-identity through group identity but also to have group support for anger outlets, feeling that he still belongs somewhere. He may accept reckless dares. As if he were saying: "I'm no baby. I don't want to be. See! I'm not chicken. I can do anything. My group is behind me. Don't you get in my way."

The girl, too, may turn to other girls. They titter, twitter, giggle, gasp. They chatter by the hour and make the wires hum. But difficulties often arise between them. The other girl gets "too bossy"—too much like Mother. Mother's eyes are imagined in the glances of girl-friends. And the girl must push herself off.

Instinctively and more deeply she wants and needs most to turn to a man in order to grow away from her old need for a woman. From around eleven or twelve to around fifteen, however, boys her own age are slower growers. Smaller. Girl-shy. Older boys are more interesting to her. As one thirteen-year-old girl put it, "I crave older men around seventeen."

She may now scorn all boys as a cover-up. Or she may turn young huntress, a kind of pseudo temptress, phoning boys, making advances. By fourteen or so she becomes more successful. By now she has menstruated. Her body is shapely. And so we worry: "Where will this lead?"

Actually and secretly, she most dearly wishes she might turn to Father to tide her through her uncertain steering into opposite-sex relationships. But often he is unavailable in ways she feels comfortable about.

In other words—

The revolt we see against the family—against Mother in particular—*is in reality a signal to us*. A signal just as surely as budding beard or breasts *that our boys and girls are growing up*.

It is furthermore a call to us to help them find healthy ways of getting rid of their child-feelings for us.

And help them we can.

They Need Us Still

These youngsters still need adults to depend on. But they need also to take steps toward their own independence. How can we help them gain a feeling of growing independence without sanctioning their running wild?

Can you stand their sneers?

Can you, at least some of the time, feel tolerance for the disdainful, bored patience with which your daughter says, "Yes, indeed, Moth–er!" as if you were lower than a worm and knew absolutely nothing? Can you, at least some of the time, put up with your son's apparent deafness as he goes on paging the comics and chewing gum?

Says young Gertrude to her mother, "You expect me to say, 'Yes, your majesty,' to everything you think. Well I have thoughts of my own, too, and in the modern way they do have sense to them. You make me feel like gritting at you. A nice sturdy grit."

"It's rough feeling bossed. I know it makes you angry at me." Gertrude's mother accepts Gertrude's feelings.

194

"Oh misery to the sympathy!" Gertrude snaps back.

But, miraculously, she whisks to the broom closet, grabs a dustcloth and voluntarily sails into a job.

Thinks Gertrude's mother: "Time was when I would have bitten off her head. But now I see that if she can *say out* her revolt straight to me, she won't have to *act it out* wildly all over the place."

Gertrude's mother knew, however, that peace would not prevail forever after. Such feelings naturally need to keep coming out. But she knew, too, that if they could be channeled without more resentment accumulating because of feeling discarded, their intensity would lessen. Then they would not have to come out in sexual exploits or in other delinquent acts which a youngster feels will hurt his parents more than anyone else.

Difficult though it is: If you can accept your youngsters' grievances against you some of the time, they won't feel so pushed into grievous acts to throw you over all of the time. *They won't feel that they must get back at you harder for increasing their list of injuries by your failure to understand.*

You're bound to be provoked at moments. But perhaps if you recognize the turmoil these youngsters are going through to emancipate themselves, you'll have moments enough of acceptance to let them see that they still have you as home base.

Remember, it's natural for them to run you down as a step toward emancipation. Perhaps then you won't feel so touchy when they do.

If some days your daughter is like a witch and your son like an infant, and if other days they're both angels—be glad of the last.

Do you respect differences of opinon?

Do you tumble into the pitfall of thinking, "Oh that kid! He knows nothing from nothing!" Or do you try to help him get a sense of freedom through respecting differences, even though you don't agree?

195

Don't make pronouncements as if there were no other side to a question. "My father never talks with me; he lectures," one boy said.

Try discussing ideas with your boys and girls as you would with another grown-up. About football, an election, whether a street in town should be widened. About newspaper items. Not just about how they should behave.

Are you a constant criticizer?

Criticism cuts a person down. Your boys and girls need building up. Tell them when things need doing. But don't harp and carp, "You haven't done it. . . ." Instead, *tell them again* what has to be done.

And *appreciate* it plenty whenever they do anything well.

A constant suggester?

"I build a model jet," says Bill, "and all I hear is I should have done this or that some better way. . . . I write a composition. It needs this. It needs that. . . ."

Constant suggestions, even though intended to be helpful, take the tools of initiative and independence out of the youngster's hands.

How about "taking responsibility"?

He needs responsibilities and he has them in his peer relationships and at school. We should be interested in these and encourage his carrying them through. But so far as home is concerned, we often mistakenly think that "taking responsibility" means taking on some of our chores.

Many times so much conflict generates over such matters that "taking responsibility" degenerates into waging more battles. Instead of the youngster's feeling that he can carry things out on his own, he too often feels he is merely following orders about things someone else is actually responsible for.

"Wash the car for Dad. Empty the garbage for Mother. Burn

the stuff in the incinerator. Then Mom takes it into her head that as long as I'm burning I should haul out more and more. So I keep running back and forth. And nobody even says 'Thanks.' "

Doing what one chooses and wants to do, that's something different. Like wanting to fix and pack a picnic lunch from start to finish. Like taking over trimming the Christmas tree. Like planning and marketing and cooking an entire meal (rather than "peeling potatoes because it's a chore mother detests").

Doing things together and having fun doing them—that's different too. Mother and daughter preparing a party. Father and son setting out new plants. "Want to give me a hand?" is a good opener. But let your child have the privilege of saying "No!" Or of petering out on the job. (This is characteristic!)

When you actually need him to take over something for *your sake,* say so. Don't make it seem as if it's for *his sake.*

All of this doesn't mean you should be a slave. It doesn't mean that you should go back to being like a mamma with a baby, following your child around picking up his clothes. Nor does it mean that you should be a meek martyr about Coke bottles strewn all over the place. This is still your house . . . and you have a right to give your orders in it and to claim them as your wishes. (Incidentally—shades of training days— a "litter place" for each youngster—a closet, a drawer, a box, as mentioned earlier—can sometimes ease the strain.)

And don't be astonished if outside-of-home responsibilities seem more to your youngster's liking. Baby-sitting with a neighbor's child somehow seems more grown-up than sitting with one's own little sister.

Do you make his choices?

"Don't you know, Mother, slacks have to fit better over the rear and around the waist than you're used to? I wish you'd let me pick them out."

Choices are independence-makers. So let them come wherever possible. Choosing clothes. Choosing friends. Choosing how one wants to spend one's own money.

Your opinions, yes. But not your impositions. Unless you feel that something is radically wrong. Then be definite about it. "That boy isn't the kind of person for you to go with." . . . And give your well-considered reasons. You owe your youngster your opinions. And he'll listen to them far more and feel much less cut down to size by them if they come importantly on really necessary occasions, and if in other ways he has chances to feel himself "big."

As for friends—be friendly

Be interested. Be a parent, though: not another child.

"My father, he has no dignity. He descends to the level of a tease. That's what boys are for. Not men."

On father's being fatherly

Your children need you, fathers. To be firm. To forbid as necessary. To permit where you can. To encourage. To feel *with* these growing-up children who are still not grown-up, recognizing their painful necessity to stand alone and aloof at times, and their lonely yearning to be accepted. By a man. Both your boy and your girl. Not alone by a woman.

Your son needs you to see the soul that is in him, not just the baseball arm.

Your daughter needs you to see her as soon-to-be-a-woman. Fearing any loverish return to earlier days when as a little girl she was less fearful of declaring that she wanted to be your wife. She is on her way now to being full of wifely dreams with a body that is or soon will be capable of mothering. Your hugs and kisses may be too frightening. They may make her pull back in alarm, even steer clear of you.

She needs you in other fashion—as a good listener. Inter-

198

ested, concerned, understanding. She needs to feel the masculine strength of you.

So does your son.

Perhaps they will listen to you where they won't, now, to their mother. Painful though it is to her—help her endure it. She needs you as her husband and lover, the partner who helps her now, more than ever, with these children of yours.

New Bodies and Shapes

We've talked already about menstruation which brings evidence of puberty in the girl. But menstruation neither begins nor ends what is called the *puberal cycle.*

The puberal cycle starts with development that takes place inside the body. A small gland located at the base of the brain called the pituitary gland begins to send out secretions called the gonadotrophic hormones. These in turn set off growth of the sex glands—the testes, or testicles, in the boy and the ovaries in the girl. They stimulate them to produce sex hormones or endocrines of their own and eventually to mature the sperm cells and egg cells.

In girls these internal changes start anywhere from nine to twelve; sometimes even as early as eight. In boys they usually begin between ten and a half and twelve, in some boys as early as nine. And they finally announce their progress through wet dreams or seminal emissions.

It's wise to prepare a boy in advance for this event and it's wise to do this early—when he's about ten—so that he won't be unduly startled by it. We can tell him that probably when he is around thirteen or fourteen, though maybe earlier or later, when he has good body-feelings he may find that the fluid called semen, which carries the sperm cells in it, begins to spurt out of his penis. It may happen to him when he masturbates. Or when he has dreams which are sexually exciting. The out-spurt is called an "ejaculation"; the upsurge of good feelings that

199

come with it, an "orgasm." And when it happens during sleep it most commonly is called a "wet dream." It's a sign that he is moving from boyhood into manhood, with baby-forming cells (sperm cells) growing ripe.

Girls, although they do not have anything as propulsive and physiologically strong as an ejaculation, do at this period of development often have an increase of white fluid from the vagina. They may think that something is wrong. And so it's good to open this frankly too. "Maybe you notice that sometimes you have a kind of white discharge from the vagina. It can come at any time. But when you touch yourself or have dreamy good body-feelings, then it's apt to be a bit more marked. That's a perfectly normal thing."

Nor do we need to be afraid that our sanction of good body-feelings will bring license. Most boys and girls do masturbate and our mention of it as normal and healthy may help rout out guilt feelings. In fact, it may relieve a youngster of the need to experiment sexually. Feeling that we understand that *good body-feelings are good* may relieve him or her of the push to find someone else—anyone—who is able to accept them. It may bring relief from that sense of isolation and loneliness that so often makes youth seek youth in comforting embrace.

It may also help level hostility by removing one of the things that most exaggerates hostility—a sense that we stand against nature and biological growth.

Meanwhile the puberal cycle does not stop with puberty, as marked by the onset of menstruation in the girl or seminal emissions in the boy. These are merely signposts along the way that soon, physically, the sperm and egg cells will ripen. Internal changes and external growth, however, will continue for several years.

Along with physical changes come varying psychological reactions. Ordinarily boys and girls alike are delighted with the first hair around the genitals. "Last night I noticed," says Don,

200

"I had *five*." Some boys are similarly delighted with the first hair on the chin. In contrast, some are miserable. "Gol! Will I now have to shave?" Anton protests. Whereas Mack, two years his junior, points to a bit of fuzz and asks his father hopefully if he doesn't think it's time to get a razor. On her side, Sonia is downcast over her breast development. Roberta, however, is thrilled and yet a bit concerned. She wants a brassiere for her just-budding breasts. "Yes, I'll go ask Mom for a bra," as she poses, chest thrust forward in front of the mirror. "I've *got* to have a bra to keep them set when I wear a sweater. But," crestfallen, "Mom said my clothes allowance was all used up."

"Oh!" says her younger sister helpfully, "If Mommie won't buy you a bra, I got some Band-aids that would do."

Some girls worry that their breasts are too large; some that their breasts are too small. Some boys also worry over their breasts, fearing that the not uncommon phenomenon of getting breast knots or tender nipples for a time (during their fourteenth year usually) means that they are "sissy." It may help to reduce anxiety if we can say matter-of-factly that this normally occurs in some boys and will pass; but that it naturally makes one worry if one's nipples are a bit bulgy and sore.

Boys as well as girls vary greatly in rate of development. Increase in the size of penis and testicles around eleven or twelve is average. The boy who is an earlier developer is ordinarily pleased. The boy who is a later developer is apt to worry unduly. It's good to let them know that variations in age of development and in eventual size have nothing to do with masculinity, virility, and grown-upness.

There are excellent movies and film strips explaining growth and development. These can ideally supplement discussions about sex. But they can't take the place of discussion. They can't substitute for the sharing of joys and fears and protests which helps children balance their uncertain steps.

Zita vividly describes the kind of boy–girl contacts that are typical forerunners of more openly avowed interest. "Boys!" she scoffs. "One minute they hit at you. The next minute they want to do familiarities. They try to get on the back of your bike or they walk along as if they're not noticing you and suddenly out comes a hand and kind of kicks you in the ribs. And they chase you in the yard and make grabs at your hair. So we girls try to get even. We try to get back at them by squirting oranges in their faces or by taking their papers and hiding them. Or we call, 'Ronny-Conny, where's your little skirtie, honey.' . . . We're all at the teasing age, I guess."

It may seem a mile, but it is actually only inches between this and "going steady." Whereas not so many years ago "going steady" was most bothersome to parents of mid-teen-agers, nowadays it may strike much earlier. By thirteen many a child protests, "I got over that business long ago."

Boys and girls in different communities, schools, and crowds differ both in when going steady starts and in what it means. "In my room," a sixth-grade teacher reports, "all my little eleven-year-olds feel terrible if they're not going steady. One of them came in yesterday with a relieved grin. 'My mother's finally given me permission to go steady.'

"Going steady with them simply means that the boy gives the girl a five-and-dime store ring to wear on her identification necklace, that they have each other for partners at square dancing and that they write each other notes like, 'I love you, Ruthie, you're a doll!'

"But misery comes when they go unsteady. And that's always happening. Some girl is always jilting some boy, or the other way around. And then the notes change to 'Why did you leave me?' for instance. 'I hope one day you will have eleven children and they'll all run away and leave you, every single one.' "

202

Some boys and girls go steady for two weeks, some for two months. Some girls go steady with several boys all at one time. "I've got to be sure of one at least. . . . You've got to have somebody to fall back on, you know."

But as girls shoot up in height and shape up in form and as the boys lag behind—which they normally do, as we've noted, between eleven or twelve and fifteen—the going *unsteady* increases. Girls want no more of such "little shrimps." They are "squares," "dumps," and "uncoordinated."

Miraculously, so it seems, as the girl becomes more mature-looking, "older" boys may appear on the scene. These are many times the very ones who were scorned not so long before by the girls their own age. By now they have grown enough in size but not enough in self-confidence to seek out girls of their own age. For the present they turn either with adoring crushes to older, more motherly girls who will comfort them and yet make them feel safely distant or to the younger ones whose adulation will salve their sore egos.

Now the day dawns for Mother to worry and for heartaches to hatch.

When Shirley was eleven and in the sixth grade she had gone steady with her fellow sixth-grader, eleven-year-old Morton. Then had come that period of superiority and separation. "Even though Morton's a wonderful boy," said Shirley's mother, "she claims he's an impossible infant. In fact, she seems to be 'off' boys in general."

But when Shirley was fourteen along came long, tall, gangly Ralph. Very polite. Very proper. Very well-mannered. Smooth, as they say. But nice. "Her father and I looked at each other and wondered whether a boy of sixteen wasn't too old and too sophisticated." But they dated. He took her to parties. Called by and played badminton with her. Walked her around the corner on Coke-dates. Held hands with her, swinging arms in time to their gay canter up the front steps. And time went by.

203

As for Morton: One night he came around to visit. He was catching up, growing fast.

"Hi," from Morton. Shrug from Shirley. "Hello," mumbled in his chin, more subdued. Head toss and a very cool "Good evening" and Shirley dashed off, rescued by the telephone. "Oh," vibrantly, "hello, Ralph."

And then, suddenly, there was no more calling. No word from Ralph. He was gone. No, she couldn't call him either. (Femininity suddenly crossing the threshold. Her man would need to make the advances. This was becoming important to her.) Tears. Sobs. What had happened?

And then, one Saturday morning, very early, the telephone rang. Mother answered. Fuzzily, "Yes, yes, who? Oh yes, Ralphie? Oh, I mean Ralph. Yes, just a minute. . . ." And into her daughter's room, identifying her own past vaguely but lovingly with her daughter's present. "Wake up, darling. Ralph's on the phone."

And three hours later, her girl sparkling, explaining, "You know Daddy, Mom, he didn't call on account of he got the phone privileges taken away from him for three whole weeks 'cause he failed his Math. That just isn't fair."

A few weeks more of wonderful dating. And then? No more. No word. No explanations. Blank. Silence.

Tears. Sobs. Down-flingings onto bed. Flat. Flattened. Sunk. Miserable. With the world of everything lost.

But, as if carrying a prophecy of faith to be renewed, the telephone once more clamored. "Hello. Hello. Oh yes. Hello, Morton! Why, hello, Mort. Yes, that would be perfect. Yes, Mort. Next Saturday night."

What we are saying is this: Parents need courage and faith. Somewhere along the line there probably will be teasing, kissing games, lights turned low, silliness. Girls boy-crazy. Boys girl-shy. Forwardness. Freshness. Hanging back. All part of the picture. Fragile attempts at contact. Confetti streamers thrown across the space that separates the sexes to be replaced in good time with what is more durable.

Meanwhile, on their side, our youngsters need us to listen to their dating strains and pains. To advise if necessary but to listen first. "Bill's a wolf!" and so forth and so on. "He scares me!" and so forth and so on. "So," finally, "I guess I'll double date for safety."

"But," says Mother, "if I'd jumped in with advice before hearing her out, she'd have fought me like anything."

Boys and girls in their early and mid-teens want to discuss etiquette even though they may turn up their noses at it. They need, also, to have it made easy for them to find places to go and ways to spend time other than in auto and movie. School and church events, dancing groups of various kinds, beach parties, picnics, skating parties, and parties at home all call for adult cooperation.

"I didn't like Josh's party," Vera exclaimed. "It got too rough. Some of the kids were pushy, silly, jerky. One boy was sort of konked, a real weird! The mother was there but not doing too well. She didn't notice things like she should.

"When I'm a mother I'm not going to be a kill-joy. I wouldn't go kazoop or bawl people out. That wrecks a party and it's most embarrassing for the one who's giving it. But I'll notice things, 'cause kids feel better when there's someone to notice and see that things don't get all out of hand. I won't say, 'Cut it out now!' unless I have to. First I'll try to do it easier. I'll pick out the big shot who's the trouble-leader and I'll engage him in conversation and take the interest of the others off him. Or I'll suddenly discover that some of the furniture needs to be moved to get more floor space and I'll give the worst ones the most responsible jobs. And I'd get rid of party crashers immediately. 'Good evening,' I'd say. 'But were you invited?' And I'd keep all annoying little brothers out of the way."

205

Sometimes the parents of boys and girls who are friends get together with their youngsters in groups and discuss "codes" for nights where dates are permissible, for times to be home and the like. This gives a kind of framework on which everyone can rely. And as with anything, codes work better if, in the process of making them, feelings are aired.

Important too is the door that stands informally open to friends. Hot dogs to roast, Cokes in the refrigerator, parents available but not in the way, and the warm scent of welcome pervading the air.

This also is sex education at a time when our children will soon be thinking of making a home of their own.

15 | Almost Grown Up

Yes. This is the last chapter. So, if you whose children are almost grown up have turned to it first, please turn back.

You want to understand your almost-grown-up son and daughter. You want to bring to them the kind of sympathetic, sensitive meeting of minds that they need in the final stage of the sex education you give them. To do this most meaningfully, you will need to understand not only the present but also the past. The emotionally important events that have occurred even in infancy are important still.

So, close the book gently. And raise the cover. And read from the beginning where it says: "Please don't skip."

A Sounding Board Needed

An entrancing sixteen-year-old complained that her parents had never told her anything about the things she wanted to know. Her mother on the other hand professed that she had "told Anita everything."

"But," said Anita, "I don't want only to know about sex, I want to know about being sexy."

Actually this is what is of greatest concern to both parents and youth.

How far to go? Or not to go?

How to handle one's sexual feelings?

How to manage the anxieties about sex and self that creep up from the feelings and fantasies of childhood? To feel that one can have self-respect and a sense of being a "good," not a "bad," person when body-feelings sweep through to one's core?

"Not how do people have intercourse, but how about *me?* And how about the other person involved in the picture? The two of us and the excitement and quiet, the high moments between us? The sense of intimacy that we essentially yearn for? How to reach forward toward this?"

Not "How was I born?" But "How will it be for me to give birth?"

Our boys and girls want still to discuss things with an adult in whom they have confidence. They want to get a kind of sense of themselves and what they are feeling and doing, not only from other young people but from someone whom they consider wiser. Often, however, they do this more readily now with a person outside the family—with a clergyman, doctor, psychotherapist, or teacher. But they will turn with open honesty only to one who believes truly that their sexual feelings are human and "good."

Warning and condemnation are not what they are after. Threats will make them shrink back from us. What they most frequently are seeking is not how to crush or lessen or stamp out sexual feelings but how to steer them into appropriate acts.

Having "Good" Sexual Experiences

As they move on in their upper teens, our boys and girls are going to get most of their sex education from each other. Although they will have plenty of talk about sex (this is only natural!), their chief means of sex education will not come from the spreading of information. The emotional attachments and the experiences in body-feelings will, again, teach them far more.

From the testing, teasing days with each other, from the

pulling-back shy days, from the overbold days of defying fears, they will evolve, we hope, a confident and secure sense of being able to be with and feel with a chosen person of the opposite sex. Meanwhile, normally, most boys and girls will go through

Father to Mother: "Does a good-night kiss *have* to last *all* night?"

a series of choices. And the shifting relationships and the sexual-emotional attachments that these entail will play their part. They are forerunners and "preparers." They will help each sex to know and be more at home with the opposite sex.

And so, as one high school teacher said to his senior class,

"They should be *good* experiences. Just as good as they can possibly be."

Young people need us often to help them see the real meaning of this.

"Our seventeen- and eighteen-year-olds discuss various personal concerns and personal feelings freely in Senior Problems Class," Mr. Strathmore recounted. "If sex doesn't come up by itself, I open the door by saying, 'Sexual matters need discussing too. They're mighty important for people your age.'

"Usually they get into it gradually. But this last class started off with a bang.

" 'What do you think of sex experiences before marriage?' was the first question asked.

" 'I think they should be good experiences,' I replied.

"Laura said, 'I know a man who says he wants a girl who's had good experience, then he won't have to teach her.'

"They laughed—too hard. You could hear the embarrassment in it. 'I think that's terrible.' ... 'No.' ... 'Yes.' ... And from amid the clatter, very clear, '*I* think two people who love can teach each other.' ... 'You have to anyway. My Dad says there's always an adjustment period between any two people, no matter how much experience each has had.'

" 'Certainly if you went to a prostitute it wouldn't be the same as with your girl. You wouldn't have to consider her. There'd be no real sharing. You'd be just as much by yourself. You'd be using her body like a ... like a ... hand or something. And the most important thing is being together. That's the way you feel when you neck with someone you like. Much different than if you get drawn in somehow with someone you don't.' ... 'You said it. That's so right.'

"I pointed out that they had begun by taking the word *experience* to mean just one thing but that now they were broadening it.

210

" 'I see. You mean sex experiences include holding hands even. Would you call that a good experience?' one asked.

" 'I'd call it a humdinger,' another put in.

" 'And kissing, that's a better one.'

" 'Depending on whom you're with.'

" 'But,' with scorn and an attempt at unconcern mingling, 'our parents don't even want us to *pet*.'

" 'When you pet, they say, how will you know when to stop? You might lose your head, they say.' . . . 'Don't they trust us?' . . . 'That makes me so mad.' . . . 'Makes me want to go ahead just to show them.'

" 'Only if you did it for revenge, would that be a good experience?'

" 'No, just a lousy channel for hostility, if you ask me!' (We'd talked about channeling hostility often before.)

"They decided as they went on that some of the qualities of good experiences were those that made you feel good inside yourself, that didn't make you feel low and guilty—shattering self-regard. Good experiences shouldn't hurt anyone. And they shouldn't be so out of line with society that they run the risk of getting you into trouble. 'And it is risky,' said Elmer. 'The cops are always after you. My cousin and his girl got picked up. They'd gone too far in the back of the car. It's against the law till you're married.' . . . 'Not in some countries. It's the custom.' . . . 'Boy, I wish I lived there!'

"You want to go ahead, naturally," I said. And as soon as I'd said it, you could hear the "naturally" echoing from all parts of the room. And somehow, the little shafts of belligerence I'd gotten from here and there suddenly went.

"We were on base. All working together. Talking to feelings. About feelings. With feelings, as always, the most important consideration if reason is ever really to step in."

"Most boys and girls want to go ahead. That's natural. They came out with it, this bunch. Just as many others have done. But, if they're honest, they have anxieties about it. If they're honest, they don't usually, in our culture, really believe undividedly that it's right. 'I've got a kind of built-in stop signal,' said Paul.

"Perhaps when they get older they will or they won't go ahead, depending on their backgrounds and on many feelings and fantasies they carry with them from the time they were small. But for now, even though the wish is strong, there is much inner hesitation. And yet this makes them angry. 'You get angry,' I said, 'because people tell you you can't. Angry at parents who tell you you can't. Angry that there should be these curbs both in society and inside of yourselves.'

"And again there was a volley of comments and feelings. But the anger could be endured better now because of their having had the chance to get at it straightforwardly and to know that neither the anger nor the wanting made them unacceptable to me, an adult whom they like and respect.

" 'You know,' said Daphne, 'it's strange, but I want to be *told* in a way, even though I get angry when I am told. You know, I don't think I actually would like it if people just said, "Go ahead and do as you please.'

"So then I picked up the ball. I nodded and said this was a very, very difficult question. As time went on, each one of them would, of course, make up his or her own mind. But meanwhile they might want my personal opinion and some of my reasons for it (which I'd read and found sound).

"And very definitely then, I put in my say, *'I think it's better to wait to have intercourse until you're ready to be married. And it's best to be married before you do.' "*

Here are some of the reasons:

Sexual compatibility is important in marriage. Because of feelings which we do not always understand, it often takes a while to work out a sexual relationship that is satisfying. Full mutual enjoyment may not be reached for a time.

"I see," says Joan, "if we weren't married and if it wasn't satisfactory right away, I'd worry much more that Stan might get disgusted and leave me. And the worry over that possibility would make adjusting much more difficult."

To enjoy sex fully with one another, one must be able to be oneself with another. Not afraid to be honest and show how one feels.

"But, if you were afraid that someone might leave you, you couldn't be as honest. Things might pile up between you that would get much more in the way of building the togetherness that a good sex experience should possess. . . . And the piling up of the worrisome feelings might be so bad you'd split up just because of that. . . . You need the assurance of knowing the other person is there to come back to after the inevitable moments of apartness which all close relationships are bound to contain."

The intimate ties of living and working together help build compatibility. Sharing a home. Sharing mutual endeavors backed by the feel of steadiness that comes with marriage—this is more conducive to sexual adjustment than any temporary arrangements could possibly be.

The latter often make increased anxiety and unrest enter during a time when adaptation to one another calls for as much stability as one can have.

"And then, too, there is the possibility of a girl's getting pregnant." Many young people, however, disregard this. They

213

manage to pick up information about contraceptives, sometimes from unreliable sources without adequate instruction as to their use. When the time for it is appropriate, such instruction comes most safely from a doctor. Religious beliefs and one's own philosophy of life also enter.

Nonetheless, the sexual feelings are there.

In Mr. Strathmore's class, the matter of masturbation as a temporary solution came up also. And old superstitions were aired.

Then came sound scientific facts (most of which we've heard before): Many boys and many girls do masturbate. It hurts neither unless one worries about it and then it's the worry that hurts. Some special worries may be added on now in this time of life: Will it make me frigid? No! . . . Impotent? No! . . . Does it drain and "use up some of the times a man has in him?" As if there were marked out at birth a set number of times for ejaculation of semen. Which is thoroughly nonsense. We know that semen is being continuously manufactured all through a man's life. . . . Does it show in paleness or pimples or dark circles under the eyes? Certainly not. And it won't make one go crazy. But most important, it doesn't interfere with sexual adjustment. Nor does it make a person want to stay solitary. A person with emotional conflicts that have accumulated inside him may withdraw from contacts with the opposite sex, that is true. And he may fall back on his masturbation to comfort him. But this is the result, not the cause.

The more anxious and insecure a person is, the more he needs a solace. The more afraid he is, the more he needs it. Fear that he will be hurt by "giving in" to his sex feelings only adds to this need. Its causes are what call for help.

At best, masturbation is only a substitute. Until the sex drive can permissibly lead to mature contacts and the culmination of love and mating, the problem remains of finding some means of temporarily handling sexual feelings. If an adolescent can feel that his overwhelming desire to masturbate is harmless, his anxiety may diminish. He may then feel less driven into acts which he would regret. He can be more certain of being able to control his impulses. He can wait far more securely.

We've heard that athletic activities and other strenuous endeavors will help. "Sublimation" is the word. But the sex drive is so basic biologically speaking that psychologically speaking it does not very readily lend itself to sublimation, especially in youth.

Some people may manage more than others to divert sexual impulses into nonsexual channels. It's as if the urge to procreate biologically were transferred in part to the urge to create in some social or intellectual sphere. In others, however, another pattern may be responsible. The sex urge may be bound so tightly in old strands of fear fantasies that one embraces nonsexual activities to "save" one from sex. Fanaticism may be as much a sign of emotional conflict as uncontrolled sexual wildness.

Actually, biological and social creativity do not exclude each other. A healthy interest in artistic, religious, and other endeavors need not exclude a healthy interest in sex.

Varied activities between boy-friend and girl-friend. Shared interests. A vital philosophy. Ideals that have been acquired over the years. As much freedom from fear and anxiety as is possible. Consistent chances to get out resentments so that their piling up does not make one fear close contacts lest these be discovered or inadvertently hurt the other person. Feelings of trust and love that have prospered since birth. And a hearty admission that sex feelings are not only desired but are also desirable. All of these play a vital and important role in helping young people manage their sexual impulses.

Besides the most important of important questions on whether to wait or not, there are others that young people often want to discuss.

They may, for instance, have heard and talked about sexual intercourse many times before. But until they have actually experienced it, there will be questions about it in their minds. Even after they have experienced it, there may still be questions.

Like seventeen-year-old Etta, many boys and girls wonder "How is it done?" They are curious, for one thing, about positions. If they ask, we can tell them that the most usual position is face to face where the man and woman can look into each other's eyes if they wish and kiss and caress and fondle each other.

"Oh yes!" sighed Etta. "I knew that I guess. But getting it confirmed lifts a weight." And then in a rush, "I was scared about the idea of being poked. Like when you see dogs, you know. . . ."

"Or when you had one of those horrid enemas I mistakenly used to give you," her mother nodded, remembering the way children in their fantasies get the vaginal and anal openings mixed up.

"You said it, Mother."

Ordinarily young people want to know, too, that the man in his quite normal, masculine wish to possess the woman takes top place. Whereas the woman in her deepest wish to be receptive is usually most content lying receptively on her back. But there are numerous variations of this which people take pleasure in. The most important thing is for a couple to find what is satisfying and completing to both.

As for what is meant by completing? Boys know very clearly what it means for them to have orgasm or climax. They have had physical evidence of it in the outspurting or ejaculation of semen. Girls are not always so certain. They may or may not have had orgasm during masturbation or during the excitement of petting or necking. When they start to have intercourse it may take a while before they begin to reach it.

We hear a lot about women needing more foreplay than men and a longer time in which to reach orgasm. We hear that successful coitus, or intercourse, comes with position and movement that successfully stimulate the sensitive tissues of both clitoris and vagina. But these things rarely count as much as does the love and trust which the partners hold for each other. It's a circular matter. Out of the love and trust grow "noticingness" and responding sensitivity which make of being together a more thrilling thing. And this in its turn leads back into increasing the love and the trust each person feels for the other.

Eventually, as partners build their whole lives together, not only their sex lives, they get the feel of what is stimulating and exciting to each other, what causes tensing, what makes for relaxed freedom. And the mutuality of orgasm arrived at together is more often achieved.

Even then it varies in intensity from one time to another. So indeed does desire itself.

As one young wife expressed it, "Sometimes sex has in it the glow of night-fire and wild primitive dancing; sometimes the quiet of a crocus-rimmed pool. Sometimes I feel like moving a lot, sometimes almost not at all, but rather like drifting in the smooth joy of being with John. And he feels how it is. It took us a while though. And in this time I've become more aware too of John and what he likes. Men want women to love them and their bodies, too." Each partner wants the other to be able to enjoy his body in an unashamed way. Each wants the other to delight in what brings pleasure to each.

It takes time to adjust (as we said earlier). Just as it takes

217

time to paint a picture or to write a poem, it takes time creatively to bring sex to fulfillment. And just as most every poem and most every picture has its small flaws, so, too, has every sex relationship.

There are bound to be moments of disappointment, moments of pulling apart. The whole day's events and the moods of the moment enter. And the small whisper of fantasies from childhood are touched off more at some times than at others. "This room reminds me of my mother's and father's when I was a child," says Sonia after an unhappy night on a trip she and her husband were taking. In the back of her mind, because of the old associations brought up by the chance surroundings, her husband had in a fashion stepped into the place of Father with whom sex, of course, could not be had.

In every sexual relationship there are fantasies from the past, often unconscious. Some of these promote loyalty, devotion, and tenderness. Some interfere. When this last sort have spread and grown too big in one's inner mind, they bring about failures in sex.

Perplexities and Problems

"Why is it," asked Phoebe, "that Lloyd and I were so perfect together before we were married? And now it's no good."

One of the secret walls that gets in the way of durable relationships remains standing when the heart of one's love-life still stays with Father or Mother. (Shades of those love-rivalry days when little boys want to marry their mothers and little girls want to be their father's wife.)

Then often love must not be given to any other. For it stands as betrayal of one's first love. And sex must not enter where love is. For the beloved still wears a parent's face.

One mistaken attempt at solution at least is obvious. Sex and love must be separated.

One can have infatuations which one calls "love." One can

218

have "affairs." One can find a partner exciting before marriage. But when marriage brings promise of enduringness, of loyalty, of a family containing potential mother and father roles—then excitement must leave.

Because of this a man or a woman may become "frigid" and fail to react to the other in full or satisfying fashion. The man may perhaps become impotent or precipitous. Or he may remain quite capable of the sex act without feeling the verve and the lovingness that makes it "good."

There are many other causes for sexual maladjustments and many other forms which the maladjustments take. But what is of most importance for us to know is that *sexual failures are rarely physical*. They come from too big and too persistently inappropriate feelings and fantasies out of childhood.

These feelings and fantasies can often be corrected through psychotherapy. And so, if our children come to us in sadness over a marriage or over repeatedly broken love affairs, we can encourage them to go for such help.

The same things are true of homosexuality, which is one of the sex problems parents fear most.

We have heard that homosexuality may be expressed in open sex practices with members of the same sex. We may also have come across the term "latent homosexuality." Briefly, this means that so much of the person's emotions stay focused unconsciously on the same sex that not enough of the sex urge is free to attach itself to members of the opposite sex. When development of sexual interests does not appear normally, this sort of halting of emotional development may be playing its part. Old fear-fantasies usually have become so intense as to impede sexual emotional growth.

But we must remember, both boys and girls have different rates of developing interest in the opposite sex. Some are fast; some are slow. Some cling overlong to the same sex for sup-

219

port when emotional problems make them lonely. Sometimes actual sexual episodes may even occur and the adolescent will fear that he has become a homosexual. But these may be passing, temporary substitutes which vanish when boy–girl experiences become more comfortable.

If a boy is interested in music, in art, or follows the tradition that the best cooks are chefs, this does not mean that he is a "fairy." If a girl enjoys slacks, sloppy shirts, and a tomboyish hair cut, this does not mean she is a Lesbian. Delicate features in a boy or hard muscles in a girl are no definite signs. Nor is a boy's virile, manly look or a girl's sophisticated, seductive air proof of the opposite.

"But there's a kind of feel to it when I see those two boys together." Pete's mother sensed something amiss.

Sometimes a parent's worry is well-founded; sometimes not. But, in any event, one should not distrust it. The whole matter is as complex and complicated as is any other deep-seated problem. If we are bothered by suspicions it's best to turn to a professional source, just as one would for a problem of extreme solitariness or wildness. One is neither "worse" nor "better" than the other. Each shows psychological disturbances calling for help more skilled and impersonal than a parent is equipped to give.

Another question that comes up on occasion has to do with venereal disease. "What are they?" Philip asks.

There are two main ones, called gonorrhea and syphilis. Both are infections. They are carried by germs which are usually spread by sexual intercourse with a person who is infected. Formerly they were far more dreaded than now, since they are now medically curable if taken in time. But they leave one with a sense of shame and "dirtiness" which hurts self-esteem.

Occasionally, even when there is no cause for it, a young person may worry about catching such a disease. Undue fear

220

grows, for one thing, out of an inappropriate, childish sense that sex is dirty. It can be taken as another signal for psychological help.

Looking Forward to Having Babies

Our girls, as they approach marriageable age, may have worries as well as curiosity about having babies. They may want more detailed repeats of the whole process. But the mere facts are not generally what they are after. What they essentially want is freedom from fear.

Amy, eighteen and about to be married, went to the family doctor.

"What's it like to be in labor?" she asked. And, wise man that he was, he recognized her need.

"Although you probably know all the facts," he said, "and although billions of women have given birth to babies and have come through it all right, still I've seldom known a woman who wasn't somewhat afraid. So let's review the facts briefly and talk about the fears too.

"As you know, after the baby's been inside it's mother for nine months, it's time for it to be born. In order for it to get out of the uterus, the band of muscles must stretch at the cervix where the uterus opens into the vagina. This is called the first stage of labor. It usually takes several hours of regular contractions. Then, in the second stage of labor, the contractions become more frequent and the baby is pushed out, usually head first, as you know. But, as you know too, the baby is still connected by its umbilical cord to the placenta, which gradually becomes separated from inside of the uterus and is squeezed out a short while after the baby. At some time during the process the water breaks. . . . That simply means that the pressure bursts open the membrane that has served temporarily as an inner lining of the uterus to contain the fluid in which the baby has been floating. Sometimes that's the first sign a woman gets that the baby's on its way. Sometimes the pains are her first signal. Sometimes there's a showing of blood. . . ."

"Oh dear!"

The doctor caught Amy's involuntary catching of breath.

"Yes, tell me?"

"The pain and the blood. It makes me nervous."

"Just as the thought of such things does with so many people."

"How does the pain feel, doctor? I think that's what bothers me most."

"Well," with a twinkle, "I've never been a woman, but from the tales they tell about how it used to be, it just isn't that way any more. In the practice of medicine, as you know, we've developed many, many pain killers. If you need them you'll have them. And now, too, we can teach you to exercise and prepare your muscles during pregnancy so that it's possible to have what's called 'painless' or 'natural' childbirth or 'childbirth without fear.' I'll give you a good book to read about it when you get to that point."

But still Amy pondered.

"Mom," she went to her mother. "Mom, tell me how do those birth pains feel?"

"Like cramps in your tummy, only harder. They go through to your back. . . ."

"Like cramps usually do, only more so. I see! And tell me, Mother, doesn't it hurt too, to have the baby pull at your breasts when it nurses?"

"For a few minutes the first few times it feels funny. I think that's the strangeness, mostly. But after that it feels good."

"You mean, good to the mother?"

"Yes, warm and . . . cozy. . . . I think that's the most descriptive word."

"Oh! That makes me feel good too, right now." And then,

222

"One more question. How about this business of feeling life? When the baby starts moving inside of you at around four months or so."

"That's the most exciting part of it all. Until that time, the baby's like an idea in your mind. Confirmed, of course by the fact that you don't menstruate. And by tests doctors can have made from samples of urine, if one wishes. They tell you for certain whether you're pregnant or not. But when you feel the baby moving inside you, and when you see it shift around under the muscles and skin of yourself, it's like nothing else in all this world."

"I see," nodded Amy. "Yes, I see. You're going on. You and your husband. You and your love. Into another life that will be *yours* at first. And then, its *own*. . . . Like with *me*. . . . Thank you, Mother, and Daddy also, for having had me born."

PART 4 | STORIES for Your Children and Some PICTURES to Look at—To Start You Along Your Way

You won't want to give the whole story of sex and birth and procreation all at once to your children. You'll want to do it more slowly. That's the way a child usually wants it and takes it best. A bit at a time. And that bit over and over. And then, after a while—a month, a few months, a year—a bit more, as the occasion and interest arise, as questions are asked or as it seems suitable to you.

Perhaps you will want to use your own version, making up what you tell as you go along. Perhaps you will want something to serve as a starter. The stories that follow will do this for you.

If you've heeded the foreword and have read through the book without skipping, you'll know that it's helpful to take children's common fantasies into account to put beside the "facts" of life. You'll recognize such fantasies in these stories and you'll understand, in consequence, why some things have been included that you had probably never thought of including before.

Incidentally, you'll notice that parts of the stories are placed in parentheses. These are obviously not to be read aloud. They are suggestions to you.

You will also notice that the style of the stories changes bit by bit to accommodate to children's increase in age.

These stories have actually been used in both schools and homes.

Where Did I Come From?
or
Where Was I Before I Was Born? *

Tommy (or Mary, depending on the sex of your child) wanted to know, "Where was I before I was born?"

His mother said, "You were in my tummy—inside—under the skin—under the belly-button—inside your mommy. Not in the 'eating stomach' but in a special baby-growing room called the 'uterus.' . . . But the name doesn't really matter. It was right in here (gesture please!). Right in here in your mommy—that's where you grew. You grew in there from a tiny weentsy thing (finger against thumb, so-small-a-space gesture) to a weentsy bit bigger (widen the space a bit) . . . and bigger and bigger . . . (stretching the space by holding your two hands apart the length of a newborn) until you got to be as big as a regular-sized baby. But that still was not very big. Just about so big! (Show it again). Not nearly as big as you are now (with your hand now moving into a gesture just his size, from his toe to his head)."

Tommy looked at his mommy's tummy. He looked at her belt buckle and he asked, "Was I under there?"

And Mommy answered, "Yes, inside me, under my belt buckle. Under there."

And Tommy looked again and he knew just where he had been before he was born.

* This is the story mentioned on page 96.

"Was I comfy?" he asked.

"Yes," said his mother. "You were so tiny. You had plenty of room. You were all curled up and comfy. Comfy and warm. Just right."

"Oh!" said Tommy. And then he said, "Nice!"

"Yes," said Mommy. "Nice."

"Oh!" said Tommy. "Can I get back in?"

"You would like to sometimes?" his mommy asked him.

"Yes," Tommy answered, "because then I could go every place with you. You wouldn't leave me alone ever. You would take me along when you go to the movies. You would take me along when you go out at night. You would take me along whenever . . ." (Give him a chance to bring in his own suggestions here if he wants.) "That's the way it was," said Tommy, "when I was a baby inside you, you took me along everywhere."

"And so," said his mommy, "you sometimes would like to get back in me. But you *can't*."

Then Tommy looked a little bit angry. He made a frown on his face (expression please!).

And his mother said, "Yes, dear, it does make you angry when I say, 'No, you never, never can. You never can get back inside!' And so, at times you want to say to me, 'You naughty, naughty Mommy, not to let me get back in. . . .'

"But at other times you are real, real happy to be out and to be like you are now—happy to run on your own two legs and to play with your red fire truck (or whatever his favorite toy happens to be).

"You see, Tommy, when you were inside Mommy, you grew bigger and bigger, like I told you. You grew until you got too big to stay inside. Then you were all ready to come out. And out you came. And there you were.

"And you said, 'Waah-ooo waah!' And that was your baby way of saying, 'Hello Mommy! Hello Daddy! Here I'm born.'

228

"And your mommy and your daddy said, 'Hello darling! Here you are.' "

(Repeat, using "Mary" or "Tommy," whichever you have not used the first time because little children want to know that boys and girls have the same way of being born and also because they want to hear the story over and over—even though you'll probably get terribly bored.)

11 | Tommy Wanted to Know: What's the Difference Between Men and Women and Boys and Girls?*

Tommy looked at his mother and father. "My, they're different," he said.

"My daddy's got a coat and a collar. He's got trousers. And my mother's got a dress. My father's got hair on the front of his face and my mother's got hair behind it. She's got a longish pony-tail in the back."

"And mothers . . . they stay home all day. And daddies have businesses. . . . But that's not the kind of businesses I mean. You know what they call the kind I mean? They call it by different names."

Tommy calls it a . . . . (Let your child fill in here. If he doesn't, you can supply some familiar term.)

His friend Susie calls it a . . . .

Its most grown-up name is a penis. But the name doesn't really matter. You can call it whatever you want.

And girls don't have any. And sometimes children think: "That's funny! That a girl has no penis." And they wonder about it. They think all kinds of things.

Tommy thought . . . what do you think?

Susie thought . . . what do you imagine?

You know it does sound funny, but Tommy and Susie both

* This is the story mentioned on pages 136 and 157.

230

thought in their secret minds, "Maybe there once was a penis on a girl and it . . . came . . . off."

But that was *not true,* not true really. That was not true at all.

What's true is that a girl never had any penis any more than a girl has one now.

And sometimes that makes her mad . . . like it probably makes you mad, too? You'd probably like everybody to have a penis, everybody alike.

But people aren't all alike.

Mammas have bosoms. Some people call them breasts.

Little girls don't have bosoms either. They will, though, when they grow up.

And little girls will have babies, too, when they grow up. Babies inside them. When they grow up.

But when they are little they've got some things like boys. And boys have some things different. Some things different; some things the same.

Eyes the same. Noses the same. Hands and arms and what else the same? . . . (Chances for fill-ins.)

And belly-buttons the same.

And the place where they make bowel movements the same. . . . What do you call that? Tommy called it a . . . . Susie called it a . . . . Grown-ups call it the "anus" or the "rectum." Children call it mostly the "b.m. hole"—the place where the b.m.'s come out. It's just the same in boys and in girls.

And both boys and girls have a weewee hole too. Boys have it in the end of the penis. And girls have it just plain. Where? . . . You know where: Between their legs with the little folds coming over. . . .

"And there's no other hole on a boy," says Tommy's mother. "But there is another hole on a girl down there between her legs. There's a baby-hole on a girl. Grown-ups call

231

it a 'vagina.' You can call it that, too, if you like. Or you can call it 'the baby-hole.' "

"Oh," said Tommy, "I've got two holes, then. But a girl's got three. We've both got a b.m. hole. We've both got a wee-wee hole. But only a girl's got a baby-hole. And a girl's got a roundish baby-growing room up inside her." (The uterus they call it.) "And sometimes a boy would like to have one of those also so he could have babies grow inside him."

And many times a girl would like to have a penis! But boys and girls, each keep what they have.

Only a boy's got a penis.

And only a girl has a vagina and a uterus or baby-growning room.

III | How Do Babies Come Out When They Are Ready To Be Born? *

Tommy thought: Before a baby is born, when it's in its special growing place inside its mother it grows bigger and bigger. Then it finally gets too big to stay in there any longer.

I wonder then: How does the baby get out?

And Tommy's mother said, "How do you think?"

"Mmmm," said Tommy, "mmmm. . . ."

"Think hard," said Mommy.

"Well," said Tommy, and he thought and thought. . . .

"I guess the baby came out . . . where do you think?" (Pause here to give your child a chance to say what he thinks. If his guess is not correct say so, just as Tommy's mother does below. Then give him a chance to guess again. And when he's through with his guessing, go on with the story. If your child guesses correctly, say "That's right! You know it. But some children don't. Tommy didn't for instance." Then, because you know by now that even a right answer can cover mistaken ideas and worries, you go on as follows.)

Tommy guessed that the baby came out of the b.m. place. "Like my b.m.'s do," said Tommy.

"No," said his mother, "lots of children think that. But the baby does not come out of the b.m. place. That's not correct. Guess again."

* This is the story mentioned on page 157.

This time Tommy guessed that the baby came out of where the belly-button is (the "navel" they call it).

"No," said his mother, "lots of children think that. But the baby does not come out through the belly-button or navel. Guess again . . . and again. . . .

"No, none of that is correct," said his mother. "The baby does not come out through the b.m. place, nor . . . nor . . . (repeating any of the unreal things your child has imagined). And the mother doesn't burst open through the belly-button or anywhere else. And she doesn't have to have any hole made anywhere because she has one already."

"But there's no zipper on Mommy's tummy. And there's no other place that I know of," Tommy said.

"No other place on a boy," said Mother, "but there is on a girl."

"Remember? A boy has a weewee hole. And so has a girl.

"And a boy has a b.m. hole where the b.m.'s come out. And so has a girl. And the b.m. place (called the anus or rectum) can stretch some, as you know, but not enough for a baby to come through.

"But a girl has a baby-hole too. A special, stretchy baby-hole, like a little tunnel. It's *very* stretchy so when she grows up it *can* stretch big enough for the baby to come through when the baby is born. And then it can go back to the way it was."

"Oh, it can unstretch," said Tommy. "I see! When the baby's ready it stretches to let the baby out and then it unstretches back."

"Yes," said his mother. "Yes, that's the way it is with a baby. That's the way it was with you, too. And so when you were ready to be born, you felt, I guess, that that baby growing room inside your mommy was too crowded and small. You were all folded over, sort of round like the roundish place

234

you were growing in and you wanted the big wide world to uncurl in. You wanted to reach out your arms and to wiggle your toes and kick your feet. So out you came. Out through the stretchy baby-tunnel (called the vagina) with its stretchy opening. And you stretched your arms wide and kicked your feet and wriggled your toes. You were so glad to be born."

IV | Inside the Mother
The Baby Grows Bigger and Bigger *

 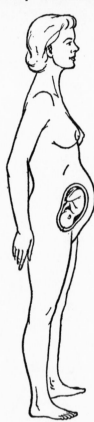 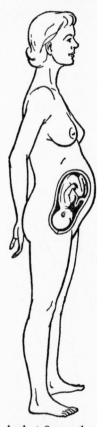

When the baby had grown about 3 months, it would look something like this.

At 6 months, it would have grown bigger.

And at 8 months, still bigger. And the mother's body would have stretched bigger so the baby could be comfortable inside.

* This story was mentioned on page 157.

If your mother were standing in front of you with her side turned toward you, and *if* the outside part of her were like a window you could look through instead of solid muscle and skin, and—IF a baby happened to be growing inside her— then—this is what you would see.

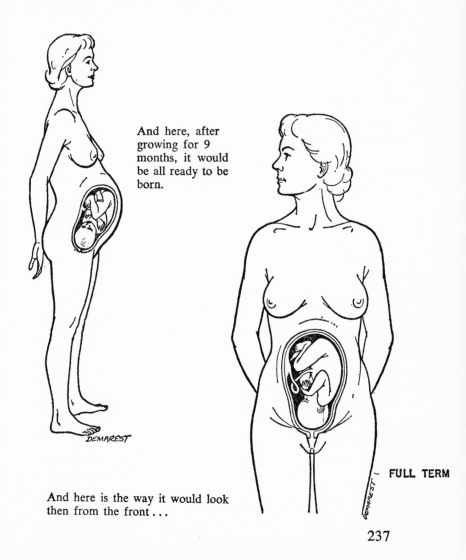

And here, after growing for 9 months, it would be all ready to be born.

And here is the way it would look then from the front...

FULL TERM

V | A Picture Story of a Baby's Birth *

Did you know that a baby usually comes headfirst? The tip-top of its head shows. Then more of its head, its little face down. The mother lies on her back, her knees up, spread apart, so that her vagina can stretch open wider for the baby to come through. And the doctor stands ready to steer the baby with kind, helpful hands. Here you can see the baby being born.

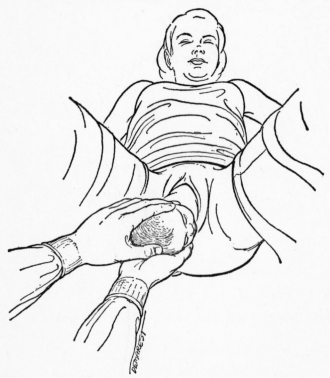

* This story was mentioned on page 157.

It has turned onto its side so its shoulders could come through more easily. You can see its head here—all the way out. See its eyes and nose and mouth? This baby has hair. Some babies do; some babies don't. Aren't you curious: Is it a boy or a girl?

There now you see! The baby is all the way out. And it's a boy.

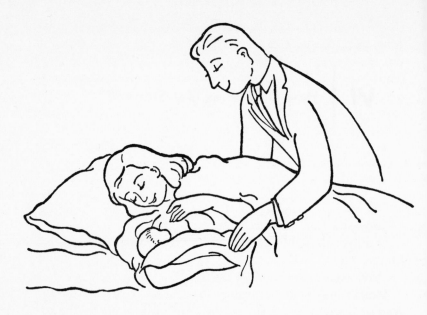

Now the baby is in bed with his mother. The mother is feeding the baby milk from her breast. And the father is smiling at them both with love in his eyes.

VI | How Do Babies Get Started?*

"How did I get started?" Tommy asked.

"You got started by Daddy and Mother loving each other," Mother said.

"You mean when you hug and kiss?"

Mother answered, "Hugging and kissing is part of loving. And so is having a home together. And so is going to bed together at night."

"You see, Tommy," his mother went on, "once upon a time before you were born, Daddy and I met each other.

"And Daddy said, 'Hello . . . Mary.'

"And Mother said, 'Hello . . . Tom.'

"And they got to know each other better and better. They walked together. And they laughed together. And they talked and argued together. And once in awhile they fought together; and made up. And they got so they wanted to be closer and closer. Until one day Daddy said, 'Will you marry me?' And Mother said, 'Yes.' And so they got married and were husband and wife."

"And then?"

"And then, they got a home together. And they put lots of things they liked together into their home. They put in

* This story was mentioned on page 159.

the chairs and the . . . beds, and the. . . ." (Let the child fill in.)

"And then?"

"And then, they walked together some more. And they laughed together some more. And they talked together some more. And since they were married, they went to bed together too at night. And they loved each other in the very special private way that is a part of the loving that husbands and wives give each other. With their bodies very close."

"Like when they dance?" asked Tommy.

"Yes, only closer. Because when daddies and mothers love each other they want to get as close together as they can. And the closest is when the father puts his penis in the mother's body in that special place called the vagina (you know, you've called it the baby-hole)."

"Oh!" said Tommy. "They do it for love. And sometimes they do it to have a baby?"

"Yes," nodded Mother, "indeed they do."

"Tell me more about it," Tommy asked.

"Well," said Mother, "They both said to each other, 'Let's have a baby!' And 'Yes,' they said, 'that would be the best thing of all. . . .' And Daddy said, 'I've got enough money, too, from my work to get the baby just what it needs.' "

"That was good," Tommy nodded, "Because a baby needs diapers. And it needs blankets. And it needs. . . ." (Let your child or children fill in.) "And it needs a baby bed too."

"And then, since the Mother and Daddy were all ready, they got the baby started."

"And," said Tommy with a wide, wide grin, "the baby came. And I know all right who that baby was. He was . . . *me!*"

More About How Babies Start *

"You know," said Tommy's mother, "Before you started to grow into a baby inside me, you were in two places. That sounds very funny, because now you can only be in one place at a time. But then, before you started to grow into a baby, half of you was inside your mother. And the other half was inside your father."

"And then they loved each other very much. And they got very close," Tommy remembered because his mother had told him before. "And the father put his penis in the mother's baby-hole vagina. . . ."

"And then some little tiny, tiny so-small-you-can't-see-them things called sperm cells came out from the father's penis and went up into the mother's vagina and up still further and one of them met the part of you called the egg cell that was already inside your mother traveling towards the uterus or baby-growing room. And the father-cell or baby-making sperm cell and the mother-cell or baby-making egg cell joined together. They made just one baby cell together—the way two drops of water run together and make one single drop."

Tommy wanted to know: "Did the daddy weewee into the mother to make the sperm cell go in her?"

"Lots of children think that's what happens," his mother

* This is the story mentioned on page 159.

answered, "but it really isn't. Sperm cells swim like tiny, tiny polliwogs, too small to see, in a special kind of fluid called semen. The semen comes out through the same place as the weewee or urine (that's the grown-up name). But the urine and semen never come out together. When the father and mother are loving, the semen has the right of way.

"The egg cell in your mother would never have been able to develop into a baby by itself. The sperm cell in your father would never have been able to develop alone. But when the two became one together, then they could start to grow and develop into a baby. And that's just what happened to get you started growing into you."

VIII | The Parts of the Body
That Help Make the Baby

In this chapter are pictures of a man's body and a woman's body, showing the main parts that help make the baby.*

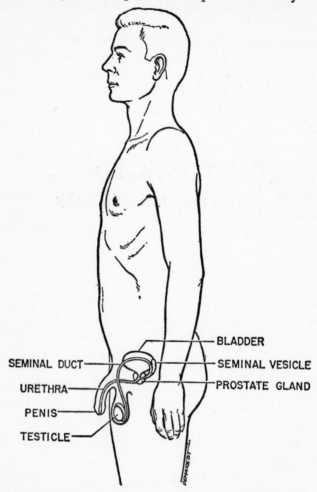

SEMINAL DUCT
BLADDER
SEMINAL VESICLE
URETHRA
PROSTATE GLAND
PENIS
TESTICLE

Between the man's legs in each little pouch of a double bag (called the *scrotum*), you will see a little oblong ball. (These are called the *testicles*.) They are the *manufacturing* places. They keep manufacturing hundreds of millions of sperm cells.

* This is the picture sequence mentioned on page 161.

The sperm cells travel from the testicles to the penis along a complicated route.

On the way they mix with a fluid (called *semen*) in which they swim.

When the father and mother mate, the semen containing thousands of sperm cells comes out of the father's body into the mother's vagina through a tube that runs the length of the penis. (It is called the *urethra,* and is the same tube through which urine passes at other times.)

If you want to follow the sperm cells' route in more detail, here it is briefly:

They go from each testicle into a little coiled tube that lies inside the scrotum and hugs the testicle so closely it seems almost a part of it. (These tiny coiled tubes are called the *epididymis.* They are so tiny they don't show on the picture. They are *collecting* places for the sperm that have been manufactured.)

Then the sperm cells travel through a larger tube or duct, one on each side, leading up to the penis. (These are called the *seminal ducts.*)

On the way, however, the sperm are stored ready for use in *storage* places near the penis. (These are called *seminal vesicles.*)

And before the sperm cells enter the penis, they also pass through a gland (called the *prostate gland*). This adds the final part of the fluid called semen which has been gathering along the way.

Here is what a sperm cell looks like magnified many, many, many times.

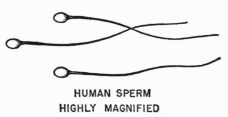

HUMAN SPERM
HIGHLY MAGNIFIED

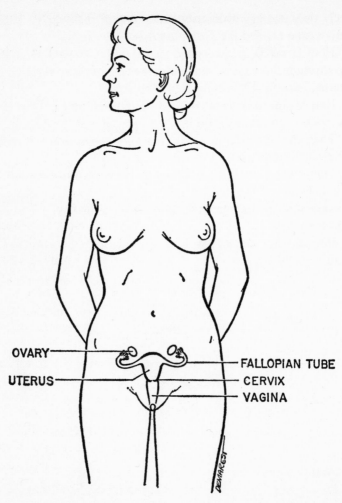

OVARY — FALLOPIAN TUBE
UTERUS — CERVIX
VAGINA

In the woman the egg cells (or ova) are kept in the *ovaries* up inside her, one ovary on each side. The ovaries are *storage* and *ripening* places. There are about four hundred thousand unripe little egg cells in every girl baby when she is born.

Once a month (from 10 to 14 days before menstruation, at a period called *ovulation* which a woman does not usually feel) only one egg ordinarily leaves one of the ovaries. It goes into a tube (called the *Fallopian tube*).

Here is where it meets the sperm cells. These have swum up through the vagina and up further all the way through the uterus, and up still further into the tube.

Here in the tube is where ordinarily one, and only one, of the sperm cells swims right into the egg cell and fertilizes it.

Then the fertilized egg cell continues down into the uterus where it fastens itself to the wall and grows into a baby.

Then, when the baby is ready to be born, it passes out at the bottom of the uterus (through an opening called the *cervix*) into the vagina. And it comes out through the vagina into the world.

Here is what an egg cell looks like, only many times larger than it really is.

OVUM (EGG CELL)

SPERM

And two more things you might like to know:

Some people imagine that the sex of a child depends on which ovary or testicle the mother or father cell came from. But this is not so. It depends on whether a boy or girl inheritance is carried in the particular sperm cell that fertilizes the egg.

Occasionally two eggs and two sperm cells join. Then unlike twins are born. (Like twins grow from a single egg and

249

sperm cell joining and the fertilized cell then multiplying into two babies instead of one.)

P.S. to you:

When you read the above story, don't worry about all the names and terms. The main thing is to find out what the different parts are for.

Index

251

252

253

256